HISTORIC CAIRO: A Walk through the Islamic City

HISTORIC CAIRO

A Walk through the Islamic City

Written and illustrated by
Jim Antoniou

The American University in Cairo Press

Copyright © 1998 by
The American University in Cairo Press
113 Sharia Kasr el Aini, Cairo, Egypt
420 Fifth Avenue, New York 10018
www.aucpress.com

Seventh printing 2018

Dar el Kutub No. 7445/98
ISBN 978 977 424 497 1

Produced by
NB Design
London, England
Designed by
Nick Buzzard and Didier Chatelus

Printed in Egypt

For my daughter Zoe
who shared the walk with me.

CONTENTS

INTRODUCTION

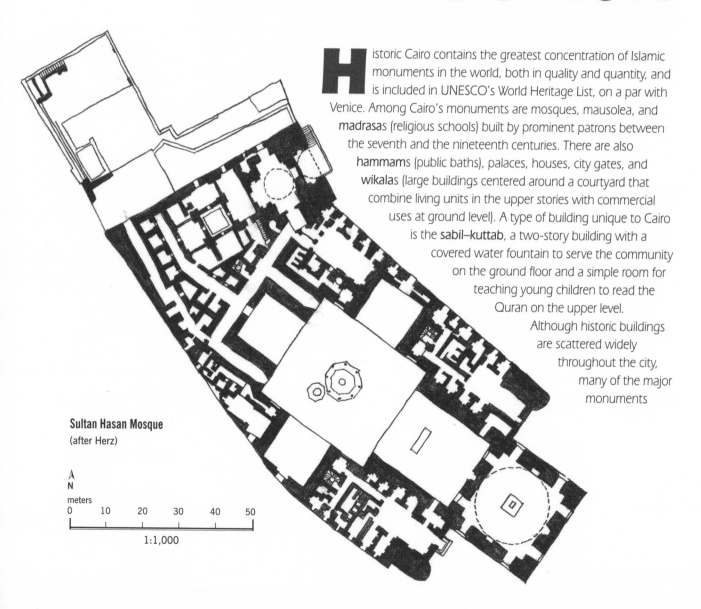

Sultan Hasan Mosque
(after Herz)

N

meters

0   10   20   30   40   50

1:1,000

Historic Cairo contains the greatest concentration of Islamic monuments in the world, both in quality and quantity, and is included in UNESCO's World Heritage List, on a par with Venice. Among Cairo's monuments are mosques, mausolea, and **madrasa**s (religious schools) built by prominent patrons between the seventh and the nineteenth centuries. There are also **hammam**s (public baths), palaces, houses, city gates, and **wikala**s (large buildings centered around a courtyard that combine living units in the upper stories with commercial uses at ground level). A type of building unique to Cairo is the **sabil–kuttab**, a two-story building with a covered water fountain to serve the community on the ground floor and a simple room for teaching young children to read the Quran on the upper level.

Although historic buildings are scattered widely throughout the city, many of the major monuments

Sultan Hasan Mosque

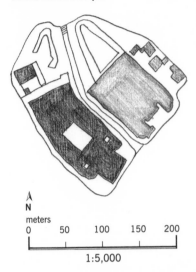

N

meters
0   50   100   150   200

1:5,000

form natural groups or clusters that are mutually enhancing. A visitor standing in the midst of a group of monuments can have some idea of what Cairo must have been like in its glorious past. These clusters create a general pattern along al-Mu'izz li-Din Allah Street, the spine of the historic city, and part of al-Gamaliya Street running parallel on the east side. Expanding southward, the pattern continues along the Street of the Tent Makers, then to the east of Bab Zuwayla along al-Darb al-Ahmar, following the sweep to the monumental mosque of Sultan Hasan at the foot of the Citadel.

In this book, a walk has been planned to bring out the city's distinctive identity by linking many of the major monuments along this linear north-south route. Significant monuments are also pointed out at cross streets and alleyways between the two thoroughfares of al-Mu'izz and al-Gamaliya Streets. Along this snake-like route, visitors will frequently find themselves stepping back and forth to various points in the past thousand years of the city's history.

A profusion of sketches, plans, and maps enable the visitor to walk through the historic city and understand what is on display. Comparisons between buildings and areas are particularly easy to make because standard scales have been used for the plans and maps. Plans of buildings have been drawn at a scale of 1:1,000, while maps of the historic city are shown at a scale of 1:20,000, and maps of parts of the historic areas have been illustrated at a scale of 1:5,000. These standard scales are illustrated here by three plans of the mosque of Sultan Hasan. Finally, maps showing the context of the historic areas are drawn at a scale of 1:100,000. In all cases, north is toward the top of the page.

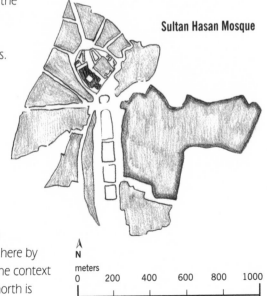

Sultan Hasan Mosque

N

meters
0   200   400   600   800   1000

1:20,000

COMPARISONS

The extent of the walk from Bab al-Futuh to the mosque of Sultan Hasan is about 2.5 kilometers, equivalent to the distance between Times Square and Washington Square Park in New York; or from Marble Arch to the British Museum in London; or from the Arc de Triomphe almost to the Louvre in Paris. (all plans drawn to 1:20,000)

Arc de Triomphe

PARIS

R Seine

Louvre

British Museum

LONDON

Lincolns Inn Fields

Marble Arch

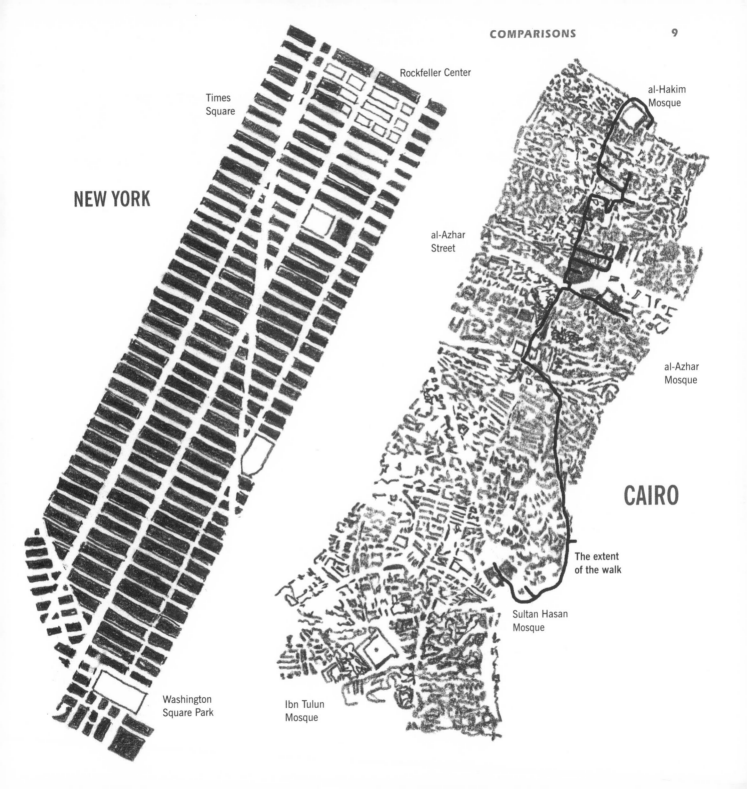

NEW YORK

Times Square

Rockfeller Center

al-Azhar Street

al-Azhar Mosque

al-Hakim Mosque

CAIRO

The extent of the walk

Washington Square Park

Ibn Tulun Mosque

Sultan Hasan Mosque

ISLAMIC CITIES

From Isfahan in Iran to Fez in Morocco, many cities in North Africa and the Middle East are renowned for their distinctive identities. Yet in the majority of these cities, this identity is linked with a particular phase in their history. However, Cairo's unique location at the crossroads of the Mediterranean Sea leading to the west and the Red Sea to the east, became a sought-after prize for successive foreign rulers, who embellished the city with rich monuments from the seventh to the nineteenth centuries. An overview of how cities developed in the history of Islam can show the similarities and contrasts with historic Cairo.

Since the time of the Prophet Muhammad (A.D. 570–632), the strength of Islam has been rooted in cities. Islamic civilization has been essentially urban in character, as Islam became a religion for townspeople, with the mosque requiring a fixed location. This social solidarity

The extensive market area in Aleppo, Syria, features a variety of bazaars, with trades displaying goods of every description (scale, 1:5,000).

based on religion became a powerful force centered around life in cities and led to the rise of urbanization in the Islamic world.

The tenets of Islam, which forbid representational art, have had a beneficial effect upon the quality of decoration, in terms of calligraphy, geometrical design, and foliation. Many examples from various parts of the Islamic world show the unity and variety of decoration on major buildings.

The mosque, with its **qibla** (orientation) always directed toward the Ka'ba in Mecca, commanded an important place in the town. As a religious, political, and intellectual center, the mosque's position influenced the location of commercial facilities. This parallel existence of religious and commercial needs is reminiscent of medieval towns in Europe, where market square and cathedral square are closely related.

Markets in Muslim communities appear either as spontaneous developments known as **suq**s (arcaded streets lined with shops); as **qaysariya**s, or planned developments such as textile markets, based on Byzantine market halls; or as **maydan**s, open-air marketplaces with trades of every description. These markets also featured clowns, jugglers, conjurers, and storytellers. The central market area of Aleppo, Syria, for example, features all these types of market structures.

In such markets, many different items were offered for sale. Similar trades occupied adjacent stalls, and, in large towns, each trade occupied its own market lane, relative to the catchment area of the main mosque. For example, the mosque attracted booksellers, who formed a section of their own. Bookbinders then had their own street close by, who in turn were adjacent to the leather merchants, and hence to the shoemakers, and so on.

In addition to the public market areas, buildings known as **khan**s (trading establishments) accommodated merchants and their goods and became of vital importance to the movement of trade. In some cases, **khan**s were located close to the center, while in others, they were near the city gates.

In domestic architecture in a large part of the Islamic world, the primary element was the enclosed courtyard,

The basic component of domestic architecture is the enclosed courtyard, around which are grouped rooms of varying sizes, with flat roofs and thick walls to reduce the hot temperature.

which acted as the focal center of home life. In some urban settings such as Yemen, the traditional house became multistory, resulting in towers of residential buildings. But in most cases, the courtyard determined the shape and size of sites, which integrated with groups of houses that formed neighborhoods. Some forty percent of a city may be taken up by private courtyards. The structure of the urban pattern was based on a controlled hierarchy of roads, spaces, and buildings. In contrast to the interior richness and decoration, the narrow, winding streets were kept simple.

Early nomadic social values emphasizing the importance of a tightly-knit community were introduced into city life by way of a variety of tribes having their own neighborhoods or quarters. By the Middle Ages, the quarter was fully developed into an urban unit, and Islamic cities were divided into **hara**s (districts), each with its own special character. Each **hara** was named after a central street called a **darb**, or sometimes after the ethnic group that occupied it, or the particular trade that was practiced there. Within the **hara**, there were several narrow streets, called '**atfa**s, with dead-end alleyways called **zuqaq**s. There were also quarters for Turks, Persians, and Kurds, as well as for Christians and other non-Muslim groups. Until the eighteenth century, quarters were communities composed of both rich and poor living as neighbors. With its own mosque, school, public bath, and local market, each quarter could live almost independently if necessary. The resultant compact and continuous layout of buildings reduced land waste to a minimum, provided a network of cool alleyways and squares, and created agreeable micro-climatic conditions. A sense of community was maintained through compact and highly dense neighborhoods.

A traditional trader in the lemon market.

HISTORIC CAIRO

hroughout this book, a distinction is made between **historic Cairo**,
consisting of separate, unique parts, and the **historic city**, dealing
with just one of the components, and the subject of this book. The
other parts of historic Cairo include 'Old Cairo,' referring to the enclosure of
the Roman fort; al-Fustat, the first Islamic settlement in Egypt, now primarily
an archaeological site; the Citadel, the largest and best-preserved fortification
in the Middle East; the historic Islamic cemeteries, divided into two major sites;
and Bulaq, the former commercial port to the northwest of the historic city.

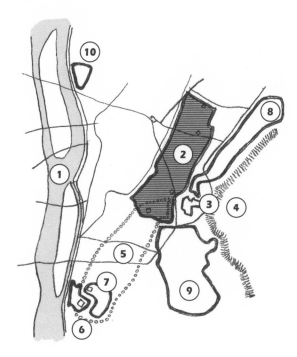

The components of Historic Cairo
(scale, 1:100,000)

1 River Nile
2 Historic City
3 Citadel
4 Muqattam Hills
5 Misr
6 Old Cairo
7 Al-Fustat
8 North Cemetery
9 South Cemetery
10 Bulaq

The Madrasa and Mausoleum of Sultan al-Mansur Qalawun in the heart of the historic city, seen from the busy Bayt al-Qadi Street.

'Old Cairo' to the south of the historic city, contains many important religious buildings, particularly Coptic ones, and is also the site of Christian cemeteries (Greek Orthodox, Greek Catholic, and Coptic). Less than one hundred people live within the Roman fortress area (known as Qasr al-Sham'). The numerous buildings and structures located in the fort are from a variety of historic periods and include Roman remains, mosques, a synagogue, and many important churches, as well as the Coptic Museum.

Al-Fustat, the first Islamic city in Africa, has remained a ruin since its destruction in 1168.

Al-Fustat, also south of the historic city, is now largely uninhabited. This extensive site began as a camp for Muslim armies close to the Christian fort. Further settlements were founded in succession, and at one time these Islamic cities were known collectively as Misr. Today, al-Fustat is an important archaeological site, representing the first Islamic city in Africa. It contains valuable information relating to living conditions during the early development of Cairo.

The Citadel's location dominates the urban fabric of the historic city while offering magnificent views as far as the pyramids at Giza. In fact, the position of the Citadel is crucial to the structure of historic Cairo, providing visual links

The Greek Orthodox St George's Cathedral in pre-Islamic Old Cairo, erected in 1909, is partly built over one of the two Roman towers.

between its immediate surroundings and the historic city. Within the famous walls, interrupted by thirteen towers and several gates, a number of important monuments make the Citadel a major tourist attraction.

The historic cemeteries contain some of the most impressive monuments in the Islamic world. Many of these monuments developed into urban nuclei where people could meet in small permanent settlements within the cemeteries. The southern cemetery contains concentrated groups of monuments, in contrast to the linear pattern found in the northern cemetery. The latter displays an almost continuous skyline of domes and other monuments, most of which can be seen from the Salah Salim highway. Today, demographic pressures and a lack of housing accommodation have resulted in considerable building activity in the cemeteries. In some places,

The Citadel, the largest fortification in the Middle East, was begun by Salah al-Din in 1176 and later crowned with the Mosque of Muhammad Ali (built in 1824).

The Northern Cemetery provides an almost continuous skyline of monuments along the Salah Salem highway.

structures more than six stories high have been erected next to monuments. Various population estimates range between two and five hundred thousand.

Bulaq is comparable to the historic city in its variety of industries and commercial premises, and the area contains several surviving impressive buildings. Most of these are concentrated close to the Mosque of Sinan Pasha. In spite of modern developments on the periphery, Bulaq still reflects its historic past in its narrow streets and traditional, small-scale development.

The Southern Cemetery contains concentrated groups of monuments, one of which includes the Mausoleum of Qusun (built 1335-36).

Along the Nile to the north of the historic city is the port of Bulaq. Several impressive buildings are concentrated close to the Mosque of Sinan Pasha (built 1571).

HISTORY

"Egypt is the gift of the Nile," observed the Greek historian Herodotus in ancient times. The Nile was easy to navigate, as its constant flow from the south effortlessly carried craft to the north. To travel in the opposite direction, only sails were needed to catch the breeze. Perhaps no other country in the world has been so dependent on a single lifeline. A magnificent and mysterious river, its source more than six thousand-five hundred kilometers deep in the heart of Africa, it leads to the incredibly fertile Nile Delta, an area of twenty-two thousand square kilometers (about the size of New Jersey, or half the area of Switzerland) between Cairo and the Mediterranean coast.

The rulers of Egypt appreciated the importance of a position between Upper and Lower Egypt, and between the Mediterranean and the Red seas, which attracted urbanization since pharaonic times. Memphis, one of the world's earliest urban settlements, was situated at the junction of the delta and the valley, about twenty-three kilometers south of modern Cairo on the west bank of the Nile. The first known settlement in the area flourished here from 3100 B.C., when Memphis became the capital of the Old Kingdom, reaching its peak in the thirteenth century B.C.

Heliopolis, the Greek name for the pharaonic 'abode of the sun,' was the religious center of ancient Egypt, located near the apex of the delta, approximately ten kilometers northeast of modern Cairo. (This ancient site is not to be confused with the modern suburb of the same name.) Cleopatra's Needle in London and a similar obelisk in New York once stood in front of the great temple at Heliopolis, where a third still marks the site. Behind the walls of the city ran a canal, dating from about 2000 B.C., that linked the Nile to the Red Sea. Thus the crossing of the Nile close to where Cairo now stands remained important and established the meeting point between Lower and Upper Egypt.

THE ROLE OF THE RIVER

Along the banks of the Nile, there has always existed what can only be described as one long, narrow farm, and when the river ran low, people died of famine. Along its north-south route, the river accommodated the flow not only of goods and people, but also of ideas. To this day, south is regarded as up and north as down. Cairo developed on the banks of the Nile twenty-three kilometers south of the head of the fertile delta, close enough to the river for water to be freely available and high enough to avoid flooding.

A coin featuring a crcodile chained to a palm tree, signifying Egypt becoming a Roman Province.

Later, near the site now known as Old Cairo, a Persian fortress called Babylon guarded the Nile crossing. Little remains of this early settlement, and its origins are obscure. One story dates the fortified settlement to about 1400 B.C. and suggests that it may have been founded by rebellious Babylonian captives. Another source dates the founding of the settlement to the sixth century B.C., when it was built by the Persian invaders under the leadership of Nebuchadnezzar.

The arrival of the Romans in the year 30 B.C. was essentially a continuation of the Greek rule based in Alexandria from 331 B.C. A legionary fort had been located on the site of Babylon, probably since the Roman occupation. Old Cairo, corresponding to the present structure of the Roman fort, was then fortified by the Emperor Diocletian in the third century A.D. and further enlarged by the Emperor Arcadius. With one of the three Roman legions encamped there to guard the Nile, it became quite populous. Under Trajan, the use of the ancient Egyptian canal from the Nile to the Red Sea was revived and became known as Amnis Trojanas. This opened a maritime link between the Mediterranean Sea and Arabia, and between Rome and India. Ships could turn into the canal at Qulzum (now Suez), sail across the desert to the fortress, then downstream to Alexandria, into the Mediterranean, and across to Rome.

Outline of Roman Fort
(after Toy, scale, 1:5,000)

1 River Nile
2 Bridge of boats
3 North Tower (now St George's Cathedral)
4 South Tower
5 Gateway

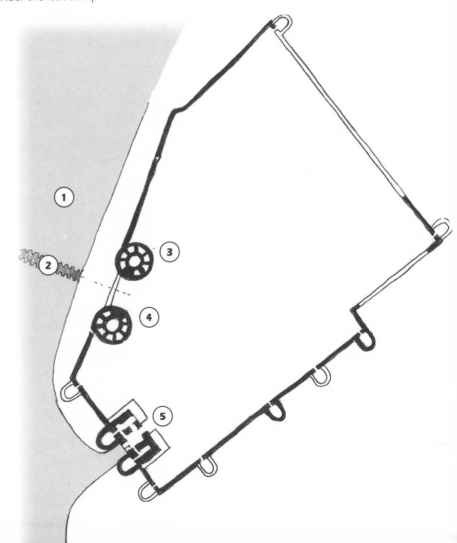

In A.D. 312, the Emperor Constantine publicly acknowledged the power of the Christian God and soon declared Sunday a day of rest. By 380, Christianity was recognized as the official religion of the Roman Empire. Egypt was absorbed into the Eastern Roman Empire, and it seems likely that some of the churches in Old Cairo originated in this period, turning the fort and the surrounding area into a settlement. Synagogues and mosques were added after the Muslim conquest, when the fort became known as the Fortress of the Greeks.

'Amr ibn al-'As.

Muslim armies marched through Sinai in A.D. 641 to bring Islam to Africa and so wrested Egypt and its fertile Nile valley from the Byzantines. At a stroke, Egypt was linked to the Orthodox caliphs, the successors to the Prophet Muhammad. The Arab conqueror 'Amr ibn al-'As, a shrewd and daring general, signed a peace settlement in the ruins of a palace in Memphis and founded the city of al-Fustat on the east bank of the river, close to the Christian fort. With access to Arabia by land and by water through the old Red Sea canal, which was reopened in 643, al-Fustat became the meeting point for Muslims from western Asia and north Africa, all of whom successively influenced the development of the city.

The site of al-Fustat, with its natural protective features of the Muqattam Hills on the east and the Nile on the west side, was based on guidelines laid down by 'Umar ibn al-Khattab, the second of the Orthodox caliphs. Initially a camp for the invading army, its name was derived from the Latin word for camp, **fossutum**, by way of the Greek **fossaton**. To avoid tribal conflicts, 'Amr ibn al-'As formed ethnic quarters by assigning a separate site to each clan in his army. Each was divided from the others by large expanses of unoccupied land, creating irregularly shaped quarters that eventually merged into a single entity. At that time, al-Fustat was a struggling colony of meager houses and mean hovels.

CRADLE OF CAIRO

In Roman times, regional capitals such as Alexandria bordered the sea so as to be directly accessible to Rome. The Muslims preferred an inland location, such as Damascus, that was safe from surprise attacks by the Byzantine navy. Thus, on the east bank of the Nile close to the Christian fort a new settlement, known as al-Fustat, was founded. From the original encampment grew the Islamic capital, which eventually developed into the sprawling giant of modern Cairo. From its modest beginnings, the city shifted its focus to a series of merging and expanding royal towns, though al-Fustat remained the commercial center of Egypt until its destruction in 1168. Below is a view of Old Cairo from a nineteenth century painting.

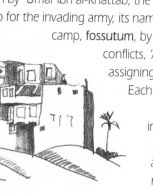

'Amr ibn al-'As also erected the first mosque in Africa, which has by now been rebuilt and expanded so many times that it is unecognizable. The mosque was originally about three meters high and covered an area not more than twenty-six by twelve meters, and was surrounded by open land overlooking the Nile. Like the Prophet's mosque in Medina, it was modestly built, with palm-tree trunks as columns and beams and mud bricks for walls. This mosque, adjacent to the commander's house, was the seat of power and administration. **Suq**s were located near the mosque and along what was then the bank of the Nile.

The Umayyads, who followed the four Orthodox caliphs in 661, ruled from Damascus for almost ninety years. In Jerusalem, they built the first great monument of Islamic architecture, the Dome of the Rock. Al-Fustat, however, remained relatively unimportant, and consequently Umayyad monuments have not been found in Egypt.

By 749, the Umayyads were replaced by the 'Abbasid caliphs of Baghdad, who traced their descent from the Prophet's uncle 'Abbas. The 'Abbasids came to Egypt to fight the retreating armies of the Umayyads. After part of al-Fustat was burned down, the armies of the commander Sahih ibn 'Ali camped to the northeast of the city so as to avoid the smells and dust of the inhabited area. There in 752 he began to build a new town called al-'Askar ('the cantonment'), which corresponds to the modern district of Sayyida Zaynab. Al-'Askar expanded gradually, and, although nothing identifiable remained, it became the prototype for princely towns planned for rulers and their court.

In 868, at the age of thirty-three, Ahmad ibn Tulun was appointed to govern Egypt. The son of a Turkish slave, he was raised at the 'Abbasid court in Samarra on the banks of the Tigris in Iraq, which was renowned for its lavish palaces and splendid gardens. Ibn Tulun took advantage of the growing weakness of the 'Abbasid caliphs and made himself an independent ruler and founded the Tulunid dynasty.

Northeast of al-'Askar, he built a new town called al-Qata'i' ('the wards,' referring to the various contingents of his army) to house the ruling class and

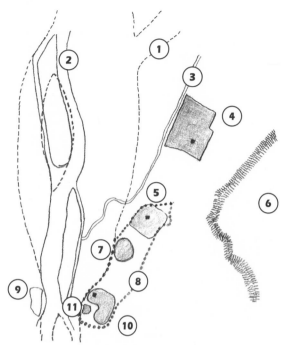

Planned Settlements in Cairo: the first 1000 years
(scale, 1:100,000)
1 Nile river edge AD 600
2 Current Nile river edge
3 Canal
4 al-Qahira with al-Azhar Mosque AD 969
5 al-Qata'i' with Ibn Tulun Mosque AD 870
6 Muqattam Hills
7 al-'Askar AD 751
8 Misr outline
9 Giza
10 al-Fustat with Amr Mosque AD 641
11 Roman Fort from 31 BC

the elite forces. The new town was modeled after Samarra, with magnificent buildings and large open spaces for tournaments and sport, including a main square between the palace on the east side and the mosque on the west. It covered an area of two and half square kilometers, about the same as the City of London. It was intended to be separate from the economic life of the region, which was still centered in al-Fustat.

Ibn Tulun was not only a great soldier; he was also a generous patron of architecture. He built the first hospital and a royal palace, the walls of which were reputedly covered in gold. But he is best known for the earliest surviving Islamic monument, the great mosque that bears his name. It became the prototype for mosques in Cairo for the next four hundred years. The mosque was the only part of al-Qata'i' to survive its destruction by 'Abbasid troops in 905 as an example to other rebels against the caliph's authority.

In 969, the Fatimids began their two-hundred-year rule of Egypt. Under the direction of al-Mu'izz li-Din Allah and his astute general Gawhar al-Siqilli, a converted Greek slave, Egypt was conquered again. The Fatimids established themselves as representatives of Islam and ruled directly from Egypt.

When they arrived in al-Fustat, there already existed a substantial city, one of the most important in the Islamic world. Gawhar's troops were located immediately north of al-Fustat, which together with al-'Askar and al-Qata'i' had grown into one area known as Misr. A new city, at first named Mansariya after a city in Tunisia, was staked out more than three kilometers further northeast on uninhabited land. The new settlement, intended to house the court and loyal troops of the Fatimid caliphs, was built on higher ground than al-Fustat, with mudbrick walls and several gates. This was the first protective wall to be built around a royal city in Cairo, by which the Shi'i Fatimids kept themselves apart from the Sunni inhabitants of al-Fustat. In 974, the new city was renamed al-Qahira ('the victorious'), and al-Mu'izz li-Din Allah entered it triumphantly as the first caliph of the Fatimids. Later, the name al-Qahira was corrupted by Italian traders into the modern Cairo.

The new city, of an area of one hundred and forty hectares, was roughly square in shape and laid out with regular, straight, wide streets and large open spaces. The main thoroughfare, which started in al-Fustat and connected to routes to Suez and Damietta, divided the new city into two parts.

THE MOSQUE OF IBN TULUN

The mosque was designed in 876 by a Christian architect. It was built on high ground between al-'Askar and al-Qata'i' and consisted of a vast courtyard with elegant surrounding arches. A spiral minaret, reconstructed in the fifteenth century, the high quality of the stucco decoration, and the bold woodwork suggest the use of Iraqi craftsmen to build the great mosque. By comparison, when this complex was completed in 879, Venice was nothing more than a modest collection of timber huts. Even today, it is still the largest place of worship in Cairo, covering an area of nearly three hectares.

Significantly, unlike other cities built by Muslims, the center of the town was dominated not by the mosque, but by the palace, which covered some twenty percent of the city's total area. A wide central space separated the palace of al-Mu'izz from the smaller one on the west side built for his son al-'Aziz. A further twenty percent of the city was devoted to open space. On the east side of the palace, large pre-existing grounds for horse-riding were incorporated into the new city plan to become the royal park. Another large central space on the west side provided for military parades and religious gatherings. South of the palace, on a site that once contained a Coptic convent, al-Azhar ('the radiant') was built as the new congregational mosque and Shi'i university. (Ironically, al-Azhar later became one of the great centers of Sunni learning.) Specific groups of people were given the remaining sixty percent of the land to build living quarters that formed a defensive belt around the palace and the royal gardens.

The only surviving building of this founding period is the al-Azhar mosque, substantially modified over the years, together with the theological college established in 989. Al-Azhar retained its reputation as the greatest teaching institution in the Islamic world for more than a thousand years. Construction on the large al-Hakim mosque at the north of the city, now practically rebuilt after remaining a romantic ruin for centuries, started as early as 990. The Fatimids, who buried their noble dead within the city rather than in the traditional cemetery close to al-Fustat, also built a number of mausolea that added to the architectural richness of al-Qahira. For the first time a distinctive architectural style was created that set high standards for buildings over the centuries to come in the historic city.

The two cities of al-Fustat and al-Qahira lived distinct and separate lives, even though they

SHI'I AND SUNNI

The Fatimids' realm reached from the Maghrib (northwest Africa) to the Red Sea, Yemen, and the Hijaz in Arabia. They traced their descent from the Prophet's daughter Fatima and her husband 'Ali. The Fatimids were *Shi'i* (from *Shi'at 'Ali*, or 'the party of 'Ali'). They believed hereditary succession to the caliphate should be through divine leaders drawn from the Prophet's family. In contrast, the *Sunnis* (from the term *sunna*, meaning 'the path of the Prophet'), who made up the other, larger branch of Islam, favored succession by consensus.

The Fatimid City of al-Qahira
(after P. Ravaisse; scale, 1:20,000)

1 Bab al-Qantara
2 Bab al-Futuh
3 Canal
4 al-Hakim Mosque
5 Bab al-Nasr
6 al-Bab al-Jadid
7 al-Azhar Mosque
8 al-'Aziz Palace
9 al-Mu'izz Palace
10 Garden
11 Bab al-Barqiyya
12 al-Bab al-Mahruq
13 Bab al-Khokha
14 Bab al-Saada
15 Walls of Gawhar al-Siqilli
16 Walls of Badr al-Gamali
17 Bab Zuwayla
18 Bab Farag

were within walking distance of each other. Al-Qahira was the seat of the caliph and contained his entourage, his loyal troops, and his honored companions and guests. Indeed, common people at that time could only enter the royal city by special permit. During the first 120 years of Fatimid rule, al-Qahira remained a princely 'suburb,' not unlike the Forbidden City of Peking (eighty hectares). In contrast, al-Fustat was a commercial and financial center, where easy-going people lived in a multi-ethnic society.

In al-Fustat, well-off people lived in five-story buildings of brick and mortar with running water and a developed drainage system. Along winding alleys and behind blank walls were placed irregularly shaped houses with internal courtyards and, sometimes, fountains. The city also contained factories and workshops, while local baths became the focus for public life. The built-up area was probably about a hundred hectares, with little evidence of public open space, although there were places for goats and sheep to graze, areas for spreading dyed cloth, and

The scene outside the Fatimid gate, Bab al-Futuh (built 1087), with the bustle of local traders, still evident to this day.

THE SOPHISTICATED EAST

By the end of the eleventh century, the Islamic world, together with the Byzantine empire, offered flourishing civilizations. Islamic culture, like that of the Byzantines, was based on writing, and gatherings of the social elite featured recitations of poetry in refined settings. Arab medicine was more advanced than in Europe. Learned Muslims had inherited ancient texts, especially from the Greeks, and also benefited from eastern traditions. Moreover, the Islamic world, along with the Byzantine empire, also provided an essential trade link between the Far East and Europe, between Africa and the West. A vast cultural chasm lay between the sophisticated East and the barbarous West.

even rose gardens, for rose water was a popular medicinal potion. Parks and promenades were located outside the built-up area. Not unlike the historic city today, there were many ruined houses in al-Fustat. This was partly due to a system of joint ownership of houses which led to frequent disputes and chronic neglect of repairs, and also to the high cost of trained labor in relation to low rent prices. The combined population of the two cities was about five hundred thousand, one of the largest urban centers in the eleventh century. Goods from as far away as western Europe or China were available in the markets. At that time, Cairo was the most impressive city in the Islamic empire, and probably the world.

By this time, the old port near the Roman fort had silted up. A new one was built further north at al-Maqs, not far from the present railway station square, where substantial shipbuilding also took place.

Up to the death of al-Hakim, who disappeared in obscure circumstances in 1021, the caliph had absolute power over the bureaucracy and the religious hierarchy. A civilian known as the **wazir** (court official) helped administer these two departments, as well as the armed forces. In 1074, the caliph al-Mustansir appointed Badr al-Gamali the commander of the armies to suppress a military revolt, and in the process, he took over all three branches of government in Cairo. From then on, the power of the commander of the armed forces steadily increased at the expense of the wazir and even the caliph himself.

Badr al-Gamali enlarged the city and reconstructed the walls in stone, bringing Armenian architects to rebuild the gates into magnificent military defenses. The present street pattern still reflects the original alignment of the thoroughfares, particularly al-Mu'izz li-Din Allah Street and, almost parallel to the east, al-Gamaliya. Much of the historic city's character still belongs to the Fatimid period, with fine examples of richly decorated façades in solid masonry. Al-Aqmar mosque is one such monument, with its elaborate stone façade, the north wall with the two impressive gates, and the dominating entrance to the south. Badr al-Gamali was also the first to introduce the pendentive into Egypt, a structure consisting of the overhanging triangular section of vaulting between the rim of a dome and each adjacent pair of supporting arches. Good taste in architecture was not enough, however, and eventually the once fabulously wealthy Fatimids became mere figureheads for a succession of military dictators. In 1171, the Fatimid caliphate was finally abolished and a Sunni government reestablished.

During the eleventh century, a new group of invaders, the Seljuk Turks, swept eastward from central Asia to confront the Byzantine Empire, where they almost reached the Byzantine capital of Constantinople. The Byzantines requested help from the Pope in Rome, which resulted in a series of Crusades and two hundred years of misunderstanding, mistrust, and hostility in the Middle East. Not even Cairo was spared from the Crusaders, who advanced from Jerusalem in 1168. As it lacked protective walls, al-Fustat was set on fire so as not to afford shelter to or provoke subsequent attacks from the Franks (as the Christians of western Europe were called) sweeping across Sinai. The city burned continuously for almost two months, and it remains a pile of rubble to this day.

Indeed, from about 1050, a series of events had a catastrophic effect on the whole city. At that time, a seven-year famine began as a result of floods destroying the agricultural economy, followed by a devastating plague in 1063 and a massive earthquake in 1138. Finally, after the fire of 1168, the inhabitants of al-Fustat abandoned the city, and its houses fell into ruin. The wazir allowed the residents of al-Fustat to build extensively in al-Qahira, which caused considerable growth in the princely town and immediate expansion to the south. The straight, wide streets of the city became narrow and irregular. The people used materials taken from the abandoned city, adding to al-Fustat's dilapidation. Al-Qahira was thus transformed from its princely origins into an overflowing capital inhabited by both the masses and their masters.

The Fatimids appealed to the devout Sunni ruler of Damascus for help, and the legendary Salah al-Din al-Ayyubi arrived in January 1169 with his Syrian army, forcing the Franks to retreat from Cairo. In no time, with the help of his Turkish forces, he took over the government in Cairo and became a powerful wazir. He abolished the Fatimid caliphate and returned Egypt to the Sunni fold. He proclaimed himself sultan (meaning a holder of secular power) and quickly removed the Fatimid princes after confiscating their properties for redistribution among his relatives and those loyal to him.

Instead of following the example of previous conquerors by building yet another princely town, Salah al-Din unified and transformed the existing city

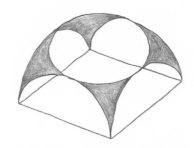

The pendentive, with its spherical-triangular shape, serves as a transition from the square shape below to the circular dome above.

THE BARBAROUS WEST

Western Europe was sparsely populated with backward and oppressed peasants. The cultural life of aristocrats in Europe was restricted to monasteries and the courts of princes, who favored courage and strength over education. War became the domain of specialist lords who were trained from birth to fight, resulting in an elite class of mounted knights. With the help of the Church, the knights became pious heroes who fought in the name of God. Theologians predicted the end of time would take place in Jerusalem. The Pope offered knights who traveled to Jerusalem absolution and assured them of their place in heaven.

while adhering to the high architectural standards established by the Fatimids. Up to the eleventh century, all teaching, religious or otherwise, took place in the mosque. Salah al-Din took the initiative to introduce new educational and religious institutions, including several **madrasa**s (places of study for the four schools of Sunni Islamic law) and **khanqah**s (monasteries) for Sufis, a mystical group of Islamic philosophers, who flourished during the Sunni revival. This ensured the prominence of Sunni administrators in years to come. Parts of these **madrasa**s were also used as places of worship and developed into new centers of theological learning that attracted scholars from as far away as Persia and Cordova.

The Fatimid custom of building shrines to deceased rulers and high officials within the city continued, and a number of fine examples from this period have survived. Salah al-Din's high ranking officials built palaces and impressive residences. Commerce, which hitherto was kept outside the city walls, was also introduced into the city. Particularly along the main thoroughfares of al-Mu'izz and al-Gamaliya, it became the custom to build shops on the ground floor of buildings, irrespective of the use above. Thus an impressive and unique urban setting was created along the main street, without the need for the traditional market areas that were usually found in other Muslim cities.

Salah al-Din began to build the Citadel in 1176 as a defense against the Crusaders and as a fortress for himself and his troops. Although he did not reside in the Citadel, the majority of successive rulers chose to live there until the nineteenth century. The construction of the Citadel was combined with the building of extensive walls to enclose the entire urban area of Misr and al-Qahira. Although never completed, the fortifications were intended to enclose the ruins of al-Fustat with a wall. The Citadel was the largest Ayyubid fortification ever built. Roughly rectangular in shape, the complex occupied a spur of the northeast side of the Muqattam Hills, and on the south side of the fortress, the terrace was built up artificially. Work was still being done some forty-five years after Salah al-Din died in Damascus in 1193. Only after his lifetime can the collection of urban areas as a whole be referred to as Cairo.

He also built the impressive aqueduct, which began at the river bank, with a massive octagonal intake tower where ox-driven wheels raised the water. Although modified by subsequent rulers, it still dominates the road to the Citadel.

SALADIN

A Kurdish general, Salah al-Din (meaning 'the Welfare of the Faith') was known in the west as Saladin, the chivalrous enemy of the Crusaders. Undoubtedly, he was the strongest personality of his time and became the main force in the Islamic world. He established the largest empire in the Middle East, which stretched from Tunisia to Yemen. He repeatedly fought the Franks, thus reinforcing his prestige in the eyes of the Crusaders as well as the Muslims. A small and courteous man, his courage and generosity evoked respect and fear in Muslims and Crusaders alike. He became the avenger of Islam, who displayed chivalrous gestures while ordering cold-blooded massacres.

The officers in Salah al-Din's army were slaves made lords. Boys, usually Turkish, were purchased from their parents or from conquerors, after which they became professional soldiers known as **mamluk**s ('those who are owned'). Once they converted to Islam, **mamluk**s could be trained and freed. These tough and violent soldiers became susceptible to art, ultimately creating Cairo's distinctive skyline, employing dexterous Egyptian builders and artisans.

They came in waves. The Bahri ('of the river') Mamluks were so called because originally their barracks were on the island of Roda, in the Nile. They came from the slopes of the river Volga, near the Caspian Sea, and ruled between 1250 and 1382. Most of these sultans were descendants of Sultan Qalawun, the only Mamluk whose dynasty lasted some one hundred years. Another group of Mamluks, who ruled until 1517, were Circassian subjects of the Tatar Golden Horde from the Caucasus. In Cairo their troops were billeted in the Citadel, so they were known as Burgi ('of the tower') Mamluks.

Their long, successful rule made the Mamluk period a glorious age in the history of Cairo, and some of the city's most splendid architecture dates from this period. For example, the Mamluks created within the city large complexes with various integrated building components. One of the most ambitious was the complex built by Sultan al-Mansur Qalawun in 1284–85 that displayed an impressive street façade nearly seventy meters long and included one of the city's two hospitals. Similarly, a cruciform plan for **madrasa**s was developed, with living accommodation for students provided in each corner, which culminated in the monumental mosque built by Sultan Hasan in 1356-59. These buildings dominate the historic city to this day.

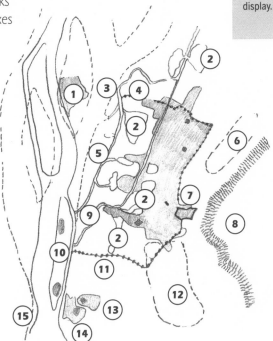

Mamluk Cairo: built-up area
(after *Description de l'Egypte*; scale, 1:100,000)
1 Bulaq
2 Lake
3 Nile river edge 1237
4 Saladin's walls
5 Khalig al-Zakar (canal)
6 North cemetery
7 Citadel
8 Muqattam Hills
9 al-Khalig al-Kabir (canal)
10 Roda island
11 Aqueduct
12 South cemetery
13 Misr
14 Qasr al-Sham' (Old Cairo)
15 Giza

During the thirteenth century, Cairo developed rapidly in a number of directions. The overcrowded al-Qahira expanded outside its Fatimid boundaries, particularly to the north. On the west side, beyond the ancient canal, were located vast tracts of land and several lakes and ponds, notably in Azbakiya and al-Fil, where amirs (military commanders) built their large country houses with gardens.

Political power, however, was transferred to the Citadel. Important markets as well as a racecourse and polo grounds were located immediately to the west of the Citadel. The importance of the Citadel attracted development in the vicinity toward the south from Bab Zuwayla along al-Darb al-Ahmar. Further south, the city also expanded toward al-Fustat.

Once a small island to the northwest of al-Qahira, Bulaq originated as a modest port in the early fourteenth century, then it emerged as a resort for the Mamluk sultans and their amirs. Due to the shifting banks of the Nile during the fifteenth century, Bulaq was expanded to the west as a major port.

Since the invasion by 'Amr ibn al-'As, the southern cemetery, east of al-Fustat and south of the Citadel, has been the main burial place for Muslims and contains important monuments from various dynasties. Bab al-Qarafa ('gate of the tombs') was once an entrance to Salah al-Din's fortifications and led to the tombs of caliphs (from which the district name al-Khalifa is derived). During the Fatimid period, it became a center of a religious cult and a place for pilgrimage for more than one thousand years. Likewise, to this day the tomb of al-Shafi'i still stands, commemorating the man who came to Egypt in the ninth century and founded one of the four Sunni legal schools.

The cemetery was actually a meeting place where people who visited the tombs and mausolea took part in many ceremonies. A small population was associated with the monuments, including members of religious orders, visiting scholars, pilgrims, and mystics who stayed in accomodation there, and the tomb custodians themselves. In addition, these areas provided recreation facilities, and many families

Inside a *Sabil-Kuttab*

1 *Kuttab*, a loggia to teach children the Quran
2 Separate access to *Kuttab*
3 *Sabil* providing drinking water

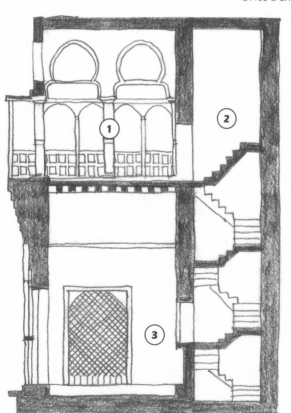

came to the cemeteries regularly to commemorate their dead ancestors. There were also sacred and festive holidays in these areas that attracted large numbers of people. Artisans and shopkeepers also provided goods and services to the residents and visiting populations.

The northern cemetery contains the tombs and mausoleums of the Burgi Mamluks. This area was located at a convenient distance from the historic city in open land where large monumental funerary complexes could be laid out symmetrically. These formed important urban nuclei where people could also meet in small permanent settlements within the cemeteries. These buildings required large numbers of staff to maintain them and were linked to commercial interests as part of the endowments that provided the income for the upkeep of the monuments. To this day, this area contains some of the finest examples of stone architecture built within a period of a hundred years. Major complexes are dedicated to the Mamluk sultans of Barquq, Barsbay, and Qaytbay. The latter's complex, incorporating a tomb, a **madrasa**, and the uniquely Cairene **sabil–kuttab**, is regarded as the jewel of architecture of that period.

Indeed, the **sabil–kuttab** was typical of the Cairene townscape, as it occupied the most prominent locations of Mamluk complexes, with many examples throughout the historic city. A number of **sabil–kuttab**s are still located at exposed corners along al-Mu'izz Street. Similarly, the **wikala** combined permanent multi-floor living units in the upper stories with space for commercial use on the ground level. This idea of combining uses influenced the design of various types of buildings. Buildings offering combinations of theological learning, commerce, and housing continued to be built until recent times. Many **wikala**s survive to this day, mainly along al-Mu'izz and al-Gamaliya streets leading to the city's former market area near al-Azhar mosque. Another important element in the city was the **hammam** (public bath). Examples of **hammam**s still exist with domed chambers providing steam rooms, hot and cold plunges, and relaxation areas. From the twelfth century until the eighteenth century, a new type of house with a regular layout of rooms was introduced. Its main feature was the **qa'a**, a large hall flanked by a lower vaulted room on each side called an **iwan**. As space became more and more valuable, the **qa'a** in the houses of the rich replaced the central courtyard.

SABIL–KUTTABS

Since poor people in the Muslim world could not afford cisterns in their homes, it was considered a pious act for elite citizens to endow places for free drinking water. Poor women in the neighborhood could fetch water freely from public cisterns called *sabil*s. On the floor above the cistern was a *kuttab*, a school where young children learned to chant the Quran. Such two-story buildings, known as *sabil–kuttab*s, were a favorite charitable endowment and a uniquely Egyptian form of architecture. In the eighteenth century, there were more than three hundred such buildings, often combined with mosques, mausolea, and *madrasa*s.

AL-MU'IZZ LI-DIN ALLAH STREET

This historic thoroughfare can be traced to pharaonic times, although it is now named after the first Fatimid caliph. It was incorporated in the plan of al-Qahira so that it ran between Bab al-Futuh and Bab Zuwayla, leading south to al-Fustat. It was also the street through which victorious conquerors paraded with their troops. By the fourteenth century, al-Mu'izz Street became the *qasaba*, or the commercial lifeline of the whole city. Various sections of the *qasaba* were named after the activities that took place there, such as the Khiyamiya, or the Street of the Tent Makers.

Within the walls of al-Qahira, the two Fatimid palaces were finally demolished, and on their site emerged buildings of new architectural splendor. To this day, however, the area is still referred to by local people as Bayn al-Qasrayn ('between the two palaces'). Near the site of the eastern Fatimid palace now stands the Bashtak Palace. On the west side, over a period of 150 years Sultan Qalawun and others built magnificent complexes that form a composite façade of 185 meters.

The network of roads established by the Fatimids created difficulties for religious buildings built later, which had to be aligned on a north-south axis. While a façade was already established along the street, the exact alignment of the interior was accommodated by adjusting the thickness of walls. By this means, both the interior and exterior areas were catered to, with a minimum loss of urban space.

The cultural activities that once took place along al-Mu'izz Street eventually began to decline. This twenty-three-meter-wide thoroughfare that once served as a parade ground for the Fatimids had shrunk to a small portion of its original size. In time, cultural and commercial activities shifted to the area around al-Azhar mosque and the complex that Sultan al-Ghuri built in 1509. Eventually, Bayn al-Qasrayn ceased to be the living quarters of noble rulers, but instead housed rich merchants adjacent to their commercial premises.

When Sultan Salim the Grim crossed Sinai in 1517, Egypt came under the aegis of the Ottoman Turks until Napoleon's arrival in 1798. The country came to be ruled by a viceroy called a pasha, who was effectively the governor of Cairo appointed by the sultan in Constantinople, to whom he was ultimately responsible. The thousands of Mamluks who survived the battles with the Ottomans to gain control of Egypt were ultimately retained by Sultan Salim. They were kept in the pasha's service and were given back their properties

INTERIOR

STREET SIDE

Wall adjustements made by the thickness of walls between interior and street side
(scale, 1:1,000)

Sultan Salim the Grim

and offered whatever they could take from the Egyptian people, so that they spent their time fighting over an ever-diminishing source of wealth.

Under the Ottomans, Cairo declined from the center of a powerful empire to a mere administrative center that was medieval in character. After the discovery of the cape route around Africa in 1498, which improved trade with the Far East, Cairo gradually began to lose much of its wealth and trade, and it lost its status as a major city in the world. Cairenes heard little of the colonization of the Americas, or of the Age of Enlightenment that swept through Europe. By the eighteenth century, Cairo had deteriorated into an isolated provincial capital, while the outer world prospered and forged ahead.

Meanwhile, the Ottomans carried out major works, such as the complex of Amir Radwan Bey built in 1730, located outside Bab Zuwayla (now known as the Street of the Tentmakers). They used floral patterned tiles and round arches and built mosques in the Turkish style, with flat circular domes. Nearly one hundred **sabil–kuttab**s were also built and decorated with bronze grilles and round carved-relief arches.

As trade increased along al-Mu'izz Street, the rich merchants settled in spacious neighborhoods on the west side of the city. Cairo continued to spread west, from the ancient canal toward the Nile. Meanwhile, Bulaq became even more significant as the Ottomans developed it into a major port to increase trade with Istanbul.

In 1798, Napoleon Bonaparte advanced on Cairo and took control of Egypt, for he recognized its strategic location between Europe and India. With his modern army, he utterly defeated the overdressed and heavily armed Mamluks. Ultimately, Napoleon failed to take control of Egypt and occupied the country for just three years. His team of experts produced the now famous **Description de l'Egypte** in 1825.

Napoleon

CAIRO'S OTTOMAN MONUMENTS

Many buildings were constructed by the Ottomans. The domed Mamluk-style mausolea were no longer built; instead, the new donors of religious buildings were buried in a corner of their mosques.

The Ottomans also introduced some new types of buildings. The Mamluk *khanqah* was replaced by the *takiya*, a courtyard surrounded by domed cells, independent of the mosque. Minarets, unlike the multi-tiered style built by the Mamluks, were pencil-shaped, with only one balcony.

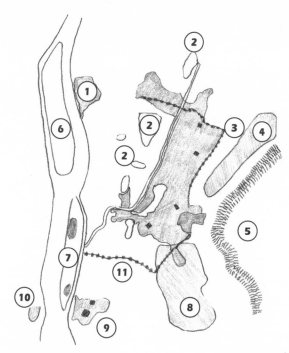

Napoleon's Cairo, 1800

(after *Description de l'Egypte*;
scale, 1:100,000)

1   Bulaq
2   Lake
3   Saladin's walls
4   North cemetery
5   Muqattam Hills
6   Gazira island
7   Roda island
8   South cemetery
9   Qasr al-Sham'
10 Giza
11 Aqueduct

After Napoleon's evacuation in 1801, the Macedonian Ottoman army officer Muhammad 'Ali arrived as the appointed pasha. Ten years later, he murdered the remaining influential Mamluks and adopted Egypt as his private estate. From then on, he encouraged foreigners with talent and know-how to come to Cairo and build a modern city, in a style alien to Cairo's character and tradition. Many Turkish-style buildings heavily influenced by European designs such as lace pattern decorations were introduced into the city.

In 1824, there was only one carriage in Cairo, belonging to Muhammad 'Ali. By 1840, he had imported some thirty more carriages and found that the narrow streets were not suitable for such vehicles. He extended Cairo to the northwest and transformed the capital into a grand city for Europeans. He, his successors, and the British after 1882 all added broad boulevards, new districts, and in 1906, a spectacular new town called Heliopolis. The city was now lit by gas, and gentlemen no longer wore turbans. Muhammad 'Ali Boulevard, linking the Citadel with Azbakiya, was driven through the historic city. The ancient canal was finally filled in and later renamed Port Said Street. Meanwhile, the traditional city of Cairo was largely ignored and neglected.

Today, historic Cairo is at the heart of the metropolitan area. The historic city is under immense pressure for change, leading to the erosion of its identity. Al-Azhar Road, a major east-west route, divides the traditional city into two parts linked only by a metal footbridge. The poor condition of the infrastructure, particularly in regard to groundwater seepage, has been one of the most important factors contributing to the rapid deterioration of the monuments and other buildings. As

Muhammad Ali

a result of the 1992 earthquake, historic buildings have deteriorated further: walls have cracked, minarets have tilted, and many of the monuments are still clad in scaffolding.

Today, literally hundreds of monuments, most strikingly intact, still line the historic thoroughfares, while liveliness, charm, and a rich variety of visual delights are available to the visitor. With its medieval flavor, the historic city remains a place where local people take part as characters in a never-ending Naguib Mahfouz novel: noisy children from a nearby school, weather-beaten, black-clad old women shuffling to and fro, men in rumpled galabiyas making exaggerated gestures, and pretty girls smiling shyly down from broken mashrabiya windows. Sadly, in Europe's historic cities, similar scenes have long since been 'restored' through gentrified façades and smart boutiques to the sound of funky music. But a walk through Cairo's medieval core can be the same exhilarating experience it must have been several centuries ago.

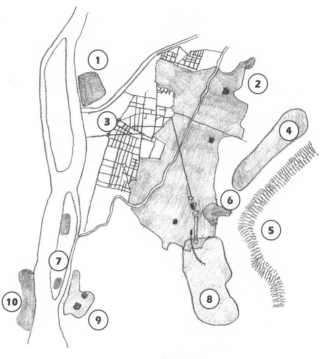

Cairo's expansions 1870
(after Janet L. Abu-Lughod; scale, 1:100,000)

1 Bulaq
2 Extent of built-up area
3 Expansion
4 North cemetery
5 Muqattam Hills
6 Citadel
7 Roda island
8 South cemetery
9 Qasr al-Sham'
10 Giza

Backgammon is one of many everyday street activities in the historic city.

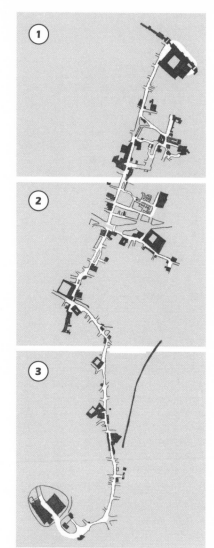

THE WALK

This route provides an opportunity for visitors who wish to learn a little of Cairo's heritage. Walking through the major thoroughfare and the adjoining streets of the historic city, visitors can stop and admire Cairo's aging beauty. The actual walk takes approximately four hours. More time is needed if the interiors of architectural monuments are to be examined in some detail. The walk can also be broken down into two or three sections. Key points along the route are printed in boldface type, while numbers in parentheses refer to locations on the route map.

The walk begins outside the northern end of the **Fatimid walls (1)**, one of the most monumental group of structures built before the Crusades. These ramparts and the two gates between them are impressive examples of Islamic military

The route in three parts (scale, 1:20,000)

1   The heart of Fatimid Cairo (p 37)
2   The *Qasaba,* from Khan al-Khalili to the Street of the Tent Makers (p 67)
3   Al-Darb al-Ahmar, leading to the Mosque of Sultan Hasan (p 95)

The heart of Fatimid Cairo (scale, 1:5,000)

1 Fatimid walls
2 Bab al-Nasr
3 Wikala of Qaytbay
4 Bab al-Futuh
5 al-Hakim Mosque
6 Mosque and *Sabil–Kuttab* of Sulayman Agha al-Silahdar
7 House of Mustafa Ga'far
8 Bayt al-Sihaymi
9 Mosque of al-Aqmar
10 Wikalat al-Bazar'a
11 Mosque of Gamal al-Din al-Ustadar
12 *Wikala* and *Sabil–Kuttab* of Oda Bashi
13 Ottoman Bawabat Harat al-Mubayyadin
14 *Madrasa* and Mausoleum of Amir Qarasunqur
15 Khanqah of Baybars II
16 Hosh Utay
17 Mosque of Mahmud Muharram
18 Ottoman Mosque of Marzuq al-Ahmadi
19 Musafirkhana Palace
20 *Madrasa* and Mausoleum of Tatar al-Higaziya
21 *Maq'ad* of Mamay al-Sayfi

22 *Madrasa* of Amir Mithqal
23 Tomb of Shaykh Sinan
24 Palace of Amir Bashtak
25 *Sabil–Kuttab* of 'Abd al-Rahman Katkhuda
26 *Hammam* of Sultan Inal
27 Mosque of Hasan al-Sha'rawi Katkhuda
28 *Madrasa* of Sultan al-Kamil Ayyub
29 *Madrasa* and *Khanqah* of Sultan al-Zahir Barquq
30 *Madrasa* and Mausoleum of al-Nasir Muhammad ibn Qalawun
31 The *Madrasa*, Mausoleum, and *Maristan* of Sultan al-Mansur Qalawun
32 *Sabil–Kuttab* of Isma'il Pasha
33 House of 'Uthman Katkhuda
34 Part of the *Madrasa* and Mausoleum of al-Salih Nagm al-Din Ayyub
35 The *Sabil–Kuttab* of Khusraw Pasha

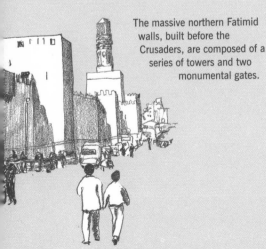

The massive northern Fatimid walls, built before the Crusaders, are composed of a series of towers and two monumental gates.

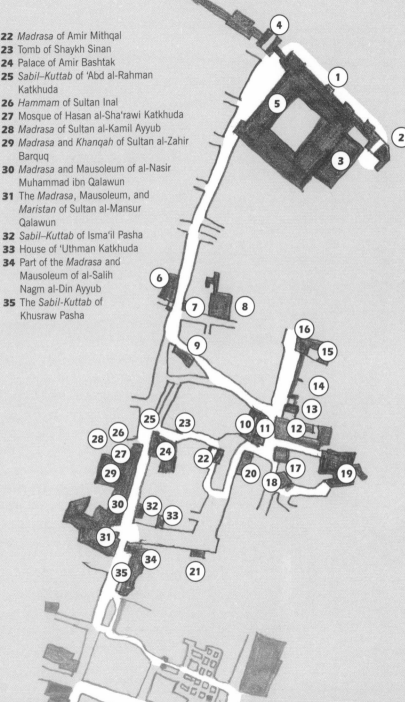

PATRON OF THE ARTS

After he was purchased as a boy for fifty dinars by Sultan Barsbay, the Mamluk al-Ashraf Qaytbay advanced rapidly in the court. He eventually became sultan in 1468 and ruled Egypt for twenty-eight eventful years. One of the most prestigious Mamluks, he was a man of strong character and a great patron of the arts. His reign marked a peak in elegant buildings and fine craftsmanship. A total of eighty-five buildings were either erected or restored by him, not only in Egypt but also in Syria, Palestine, and Mecca. His buildings are noted for their decorative details and fine workmanship.

architecture, although they were never used in a siege. The present stone enclosure is slightly larger than the original brick walls of al-Qahira, founded in 969. These walls were commissioned in 1087 by Badr al-Gamali, the commander of the caliph's armies, to protect the city from possible attack by the Seljuk Turks. The Armenian architect John the Monk and his two brothers used high-quality stone and carved meticulous masonry details in a variety of vaults, shallow domes, and round arches. Cut stone was expensive, so many pharaonic structures were destroyed to build the walls.

The masonry in the lower part of the wall was reinforced with horizontal columns. The ground was lower than its present level, and the gate entrances were reached by ramps from the street. Along the entire length of the walls run internal galleries connected by a series of vaulted rooms with arrow slits on the exterior and clear openings looking onto the city. Here guard rooms and living quarters turned the wall into a fortress. These passages were blocked at the gates to increase security.

Towers were placed at regular intervals along the wall, with slits on three sides to allow soldiers a full view on the external side. Between the gates, a splendid inscription of Quranic verses in the Kufic style is carved in stone along the exterior of the wall. On the upper part is a terrace protected by rounded merlons along the parapet.

In the twelfth century, Salah al-Din greatly admired the walls, but did not find them secure enough, so he reinforced them on either side of the gates. Later, in 1789, Napoleon installed his troops within the fortifications and enlarged the arrow slits to allow for cannon fire. Until recent years, the walls had been encroached upon by the hovels of the poor.

To fully appreciate this military structure, it is necessary to climb inside the ramparts. After obtaining the key from the custodian of one of the gates, the visitor can walk inside the vaulted passages and then return along the parapet, from which there is a splendid view of the city's many domes and minarets.

Bab al-Nasr (2) is the massive fortified gate with rectangular stone towers flanking the semicircular arch of the eastern portal. The original Bab al-Nasr was built south of the present one by General Gawhar al-Siqilli when the city was first laid out. Later, Wazir Badr al-Gamali enlarged the city and replaced the first gate with the present one, naming it Bab al-'Izz ('gate of glory').

Despite this, the inhabitants have shown preference for the original name, meaning 'gate of victory,' which has remained in use to this day.

A significant decorative feature is the shields on the flanks and fronts of the protruding towers, which symbolize victory in protecting the city against invaders. Napoleon later named each tower of the north wall after the officers responsible for its security. The names of French officers are carved near the upper level of the gate: Tour Corbin on the east tower and Tour Julien on the west.

Passing through Bab al-Nasr is al-Gamaliya Street, which runs almost parallel with al-Mu'izz Street. Here many commercial establishments can still be found. When Bulaq was developed as the main port in place of al-Fustat, goods from the Red Sea were transported overland and passed by the north wall to reach their destination. During the seventeenth and eighteenth centuries, this area saw the construction of many **wikala**s that dealt in spices, coffee, and textiles. Immediately inside the gate is the large **Wikala of Qaytbay (3)**, one of the few remaining **wikala**s from the Mamluk period. The Mamluk

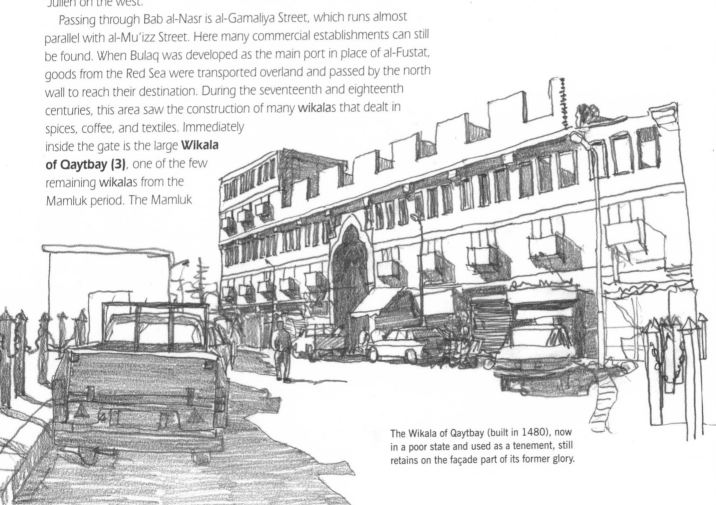

The Wikala of Qaytbay (built in 1480), now in a poor state and used as a tenement, still retains on the façade part of its former glory.

sultan al-Ashraf Qaytbay endowed it upon his return from pilgrimage in 1480 in order to support the poor in Medina, now in Saudi Arabia.

The regular façade of this **wikala**, with a decorated doorway three stories high, is made up of a series of identical bays. Shops and storerooms were placed on the ground floor, with living units for travelers and merchants above. A large rectangular courtyard provided space for unloading goods from pack animals. Although it is now in a poor state and used as a tenement, one can still see the typical layout of a commercial warehouse building that has remained unchanged over many centuries.

Return through Bab al-Nasr and walk outside along the wall to **Bab al-Futuh (4)**. Built at the same time as Bab al-Nasr, this gate, with its frequent curves and arched motifs, appears less severe than the other. It replaced an earlier gate included in Gawhar's enclosure, and Badr al-Gamali named it Bab al-Iqbal ('gate of prosperity'). Again, however, the inhabitants kept the original name of Bab al-Futuh ('gate of conquests').

Each of the two semicircular towers has curved rectangles with arrow slits that provide light to the rooms above. Over the entrance is a splayed arch decorated with diamond-shaped motifs. The overhanging cornice provided a place through which boiling oil or lime could be poured on the enemy below. The end brackets show the heads of rams, representing the zodiacal sign of Mars (al-Qahir in Arabic). Mars was in ascendance when the city was founded, and hence its name, al-Qahira.

The top of the wall offers a fine view of al-Mu'izz Street, the main thoroughfare or **qasaba** that continues right through the Fatimid city and on to al-Fustat. This street contains a series of markets, each specializing in a particular product. This increases competition and leads to product improvement and the growth of a local

MONUMENTAL RAMPARTS

Gawhar al-Siqilli, the commander of the forces of the first Fatimid caliph, laid out the rectangular city, with its enormous thick brick walls, wide enough for two horsemen to ride abreast along the top. More than a hundred years later, Badr al-Gamali, the powerful Fatimid *wazir* who ruled Egypt from 1074 to 1094, rebuilt al-Qahira's defenses based on his knowledge of Byzantine fortifications. He marginally increased the area of the city by extending the walls to the north and south.

Inside Bab al-Futuh is the first market area
along the main street, heavy with the smell
of fresh lemons, onions, and garlic.

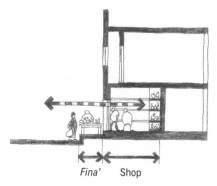

Fina'   Shop

Fina' refers to the relationship between the inner space of a building, its frontage, and part of the paved street area.

reputation. Immediately inside Bab al-Futuh, the street widens into the first market area, where lemons, onions, and garlic are sold.

On the right side is the extensive **al-Hakim Mosque (5)**, named after the third Fatimid caliph. This mosque was originally outside Gawhar's enclosure, but was incorporated into the extended fortifications built by Badr al-Gamali. It consists of an irregular rectangle with four arcades surrounding a courtyard. An unusual feature is the monumental entrance with its projecting stone porch. The most specatacular features of the building are the minarets on either side of the façade reminiscent of the propylon to a pharaonic temple. Originally, the two stone minarets stood independent of the brick walls at the corners. They are the earliest surviving minarets in the city, although they have been restored at various times in history. The massive salients were added in 1010 to strengthen their structure, and the northern minaret was incorporated into the city wall. Inside, these strange structures are hollow, for they have been built around the original minarets, which are connected with brackets and can still be seen from the minaret above.

At various times, this mosque was used as a prison for Crusaders, as Salah al-Din's stable, as Napoleon's fortress, and as a local school. In 1980, the mosque was practically rebuilt in gleaming white marble and gold trim by the Bohra, a Shi'i sect based in India. However, remnants of the original decoration still remain, in stucco carvings, on timber tie-beams, and Quranic inscriptions.

From here on, the character of the old city is one of narrow, busy streets, with almost continuous development. The few open spaces that do exist are dominated by parked vehicles, and consequently, the streets have become an important venue for recreation and social interaction. In fact, local people exert a traditional right over the street as public space. The traditional concept of **fina'**, referring to the relationship between the inner space of a building, its frontage, and part of the paved street area, plays a major role in creating the street environment. People make things on the street, compete to sell goods there, and generally use it as an extension of their residential premises. Local residents also use the street for social events such as weddings and funerals. Since all these activities spill out into the street, the actual roadway must often be used for walking. Yet this method of occupying the street makes good economic sense and encourages community interaction.

One of the massive salients to the Mosque of
al-Hakim added in 1010, reminiscent of the
propylon to a pharaonic temple.

AL-HAKIM BI-'AMR ALLAH

Al-Hakim, the third Fatimid caliph, reigned from the age of eleven and became infamous for his eccentric laws, arbitrary executions, and violent acts. He forbade the making of women's shoes in order to confine them indoors and savagely persecuted Christians, even though his mother was a Christian concubine of the caliph. However, during his twenty-four-year reign, he instituted a House of Science for learned discussions and had one of the richest Arab manuscript collections of his time. The famous mosque was started in 990 by his father, al-'Aziz, and was completed by al-Hakim. One night in 1021, al-Hakim disappeared, probably murdered.

At the southern end of al-Hakim mosque begins a new market area associated with metal products and coffee shop equipment, such as tables for cafés and water pipes. Continue walking along al-Mu'izz Street past al-Hakim mosque and pass the first turn on the left, called al-Dubabiya. On the right side just before the second turn is the **Mosque and Sabil–Kuttab of Sulayman Agha al-Silahdar (6)**. This building is one of several endowed by Sulayman 'the Armorer,' who was in charge of the city's arsenal during the reign of Muhammad 'Ali. Built between 1837 and 1839, this complex is a mixture of Ottoman Turkish and Cairene styles. The undulating façade is covered with relief carving and crowned with an elaborate overhanging roof of timber eaves that flare upward. The mosque and **kuttab** are of limestone,

The Ottoman Mosque and Sabil-Kuttab of Sulayman Agha al-Silahdar (built 1837-39) has elaborate overhanging eaves and a pencil-thin minaret, which dominates this part of the street.

while the **sabil**'s rounded form is faced in white marble and decorated with bronze grilles. On the south end of the elevation, a gateway gives access to the building at the rear and to the rest of the quarter, Harat al-Burguwan. The building can also be entered by the door at the north end of the façade.

The Ottoman minaret on the northeast corner is a dominant feature on the skyline along al-Mu'izz Street. The mosque is entered through a typical Cairene baffled corridor, a type of entrance first used in military architecture and adopted in religious buildings to avoid abrupt entry from the street. From here, a flight of steps leads up to the covered court with a central skylight. On the northwest wall is a gallery for women.

At the corner on the other side of al-Mu'izz Street is al-Darb al-Asfar. On the left stands the charming house of the coffee merchant **Mustafa Ga'far (7)**, built in 1713 and now used as the local office of the antiquities department. A little further along the alleyway is **Bayt al-Sihaymi (8)**, which is actually two houses, one built in 1648 and the other in 1796. One house forms the courtyard, while the other extends the north and south elevations. It is an example of once-gracious living, with some of the comforts still in evidence. Here sunlight and cool wind filter through **mashrabiya**s (wooden lattice alcove windows that provide privacy for women). There are also dome-lit baths and deep recesses around each room providing seating and storage space.

The house has a simple but indirect entrance that leads to a landscaped courtyard. Here the sound of running water from a fountain could once be heard, in contrast to the hot and dusty city outside. Around the courtyard, the house is divided into separate areas, the **salamlik** on the ground floor, where men greeted their guests, and the **haramlik**, or private quarters above, reserved for women and the family.

On the second floor is the **maq'ad** (or loggia, usually an arched open sitting area on the courtyard facing north to catch the breeze), where men could relax with their friends. In winter, guests were entertained in a grand **qa'a** (a large reception area). The variety of decoration is rich and lavish: marble floors, stained glass, painted ceilings, and a **malqaf**, a device to scoop the breeze and channel it through the house in the summer.

Returning to al-Mu'izz Street, on the next left-hand corner is the elegant **Mosque of al-Aqmar (9)**, meaning 'the moonlit,' due to the haunting color of the gray stone. This location corresponds to the

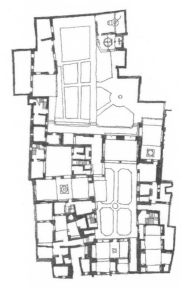

The plan of Bayt al-Sihaymi consists of two houses, one built in 1648 and the other in 1796 *(based on plans from l'Ouvrage publié avec le concours du Centre National de la Recherche Scientifique; scale, 1:1,000).*

WATER PIPES

During the Ottoman period, new products were introduced into Egypt. Coffee became available in the sixteenth century, and tobacco arrived from Persia in the seventeenth century. In the historic city today, coffee houses offer a smoking contraption called a *shisha*, or water pipe. It consists of a glass container with a long, flexible tube. Over the neck of the glass is a brass stand for the small clay bowl that holds the pieces of coal and tobacco. By sucking on the tube, the smoke from the tobacco mixture lit by the coal is drawn through the water in the bottle.

The once imposing Ottoman Wikalat al-Bazar'a (left) is adjacent to the Mosque of Gamal al-Din al-Ustadar (right), who gave his name to the district of Gamaliya *(based on plans from l'Institut Français d'Archéologie Orientale du Caire; scale, 1:1,000).*

THE FOUR SCHOOLS OF LAW

The founders of the four legal schools of Sunni Islam were the imams Malik, Abu Hanifa, Ibn Hanbal, and al-Shafi'i. In keeping with their teachings, four distinct interpretations of Islamic law developed. Until the end of the Fatimid period in Egypt, education took place either in the mosque or in private academies. When Salah al-Din became sultan in the twelfth century, he introduced the *madrasa,* essentially a religious institution run by the state. To ensure a strong intellectual unity and avoid any cause for rivalry in Sunni Islam, all four schools were usually taught on an equal basis in the *madrasa.*

southeast corner of the once great Fatimid palace. The delicate design of the mosque's façade may have been influenced by its location as a place for official parades and imperial appearances. Built for al-Amir, the seventh caliph, it is one of the very few Fatimid buildings to have survived. However, in 1980, it was inventively restored by the Bohras, who even added new windows and inscriptions.

Although this building is less imposing than the expansive al-Hakim mosque, it remains influential in Cairo's architectural history. It is one of the first mosques in Cairo where the façade was built to follow the north-south street alignment, while the interior and the qibla wall remained oriented to the east, toward Mecca. The building is set back slightly from the street alignment. The ground level has risen dramatically over the centuries and the visitor must step down to enter the mosque. Inside, the layout is that of a congregational mosque with an almost square courtyard, where a band of highly ornamental square Kufic script still survives around the arches. This is the first building in Cairo to display applied decoration on stone (stucco: wet plaster stamped with carved wooden molds), together with modest **muqarnas** vaulting, or stalactites, which later became popular with the Mamluks. The whole façade is highly stylized, with numerous symbolic motifs. At the center above the entrance is a beautiful stone rosette of four concentric rings.

Turn left at the narrow lane before al-Aqmar mosque and walk along al-Tumbakshiya Street toward Gamaliya Street. At the end of al-Tumbakshiya on the right are two historic buildings side by side. Like so many monuments in the historic city, these once imposing buildings are now in a dilapidated state, showing little evidence of their former glory. The first is the Ottoman **Wikalat al-Bazar'a (10)**, built in the seventeenth century by Hasan Katkhuda Abu Shanab. The decoration is concentrated on the entrance, through which a vaulted passage leads to the large courtyard. The first floor of storerooms is built of stone, while the accommodation above is brick and plaster.

This **wikala** adjoins the cruciform **Mosque of Gamal al-Din al-Ustadar (11)**. It was founded by the powerful amir Gamal al-Din Yusuf in 1408, who gave his name to the district of Gamaliya. Although it is called a mosque, it is actually a **madrasa**, built for the study of all four schools of Islamic law. The rent from the shops below the raised entrance helped pay for maintaining the building and its staff. Gamal al-Din reportedly spent twelve thousand gold

The once elegant Mosque of al-Aqmar, built for al-Amir, the seventh caliph, is one of the very few buildings to have survived from the Fatimid era.

Wikala and Sabil-Kuttab of Oda
Bashi is in Gamaliya Street,
contributing to the medieval
atmosphere in this part of the city.

dinars on its construction and rich decoration and planned to retire there, but the sultan Farag ibn Barquq was displeased with him and seized all his possessions and executed him.

On the opposite corner, across Gamaliya Street, are the **Wikala and Sabil–Kuttab of Oda Bashi (12)**, both built by Muhammad Katkhuda and his brother Amir Dhu al-Fiqar Katkhuda Mustahfizan at the end of the seventeenth century. The wikala, dealing primarily in coffee and spices, was one of the largest and most important trading establishments in Ottoman Cairo. On the ground floor, there were more than thirty storerooms, while an equal number of apartments accommodated merchants upstairs. On the top floor, there was a rab', a tenement with rooms for people working in the neighborhood. Today, it is in a poor state, although its imposing entrance retains its strong sense of history. Only the façade of the sabil–kuttab, with its double projecting timber awnings and panels of blue and green tiles, remains intact.

A little way to the north and on the right is the Ottoman **Bawabat Harat al-Mubayyadin (13)** Quarter. Such street gates were a common feature in Cairo until the nineteenth century. Traditionally, the historic city was divided into ethnic neighborhoods, or haras, with their own network of streets and gates that closed at night. Each hara had its own place of worship, a political representative called shaykh al-hara to settle disputes, and a futuwa, or 'champion' who offered protection. Weddings, deaths, and fights were

On one of the windows of the Madrasa and Mausoleum of Amir Qarasunqur is the badge of office of the founder, who was a polo master, showing two sticks in a circle.

The Ottoman Bawabat Harat al-Mubayyadin is one of a number of street gateways still surviving in the historic city. The actual gates were removed by Napoleon for reasons of security.

considered to be public affairs involving the community. At first, **hara**s were occupied by a combination of rich merchants, craftsmen, and poor laborers. By the eighteenth century, separate quarters had sprung up for common people involved in such activities as milling and tanning, which were considered unpleasant by the well-to-do in the community. Napoleon removed many of the **hara** gates, although several gateways still exist, along with parts of the street network.

Continue walking a few paces further north on the same side of the street to the remains of the **Madrasa and Mausoleum of Amir Qarasunqur (14)**. Qarasunqur ('black falcon') was once a slave of Sultan Qalawun and was later made a page and then an amir. He was also a **gukandar**, or polo master, and his badge of office of two polo sticks in a circle is featured above one of the windows of the mausoleum façade. He actually built two other tombs for himself: one in Aleppo, Syria and another in Marragha, Iran, where he was buried after committing suicide in 1328. Since the nineteenth century, the **madrasa** has been the Gamaliya Boys School, and all that remains is the mausoleum and part of the façade.

Seventy-five meters further on the east side of the street is the **Khanqah of Baybars II (15)**, built in 1309 to accommodate four hundred Sufis and children of the Mamluks. This is the oldest **khanqah** (monastery) that has survived in Cairo.

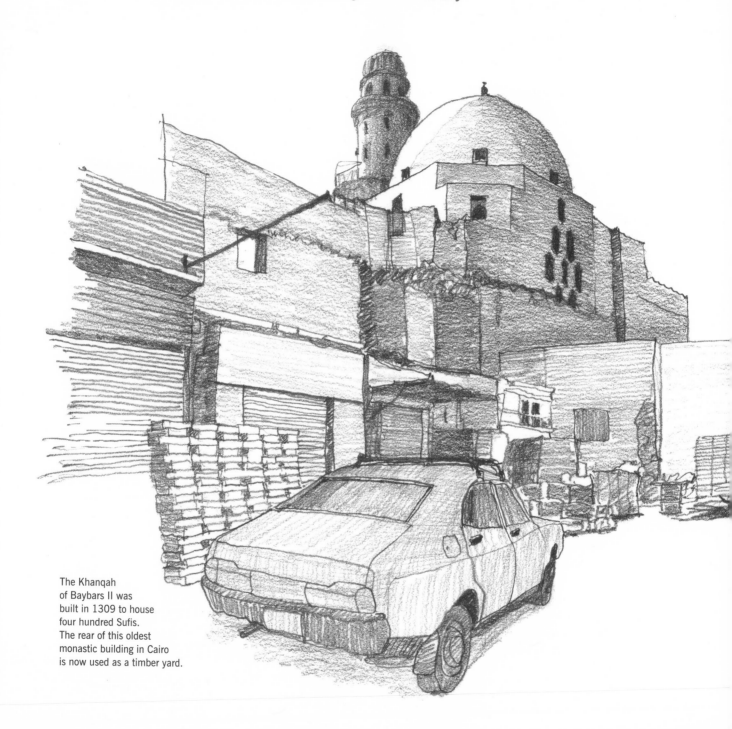

The Khanqah
of Baybars II was
built in 1309 to house
four hundred Sufis.
The rear of this oldest
monastic building in Cairo
is now used as a timber yard.

Baybars II, known as al-Gashankir ('the taster,' a court position he held at one point) decorated the building lavishly. Within the confines of the irregular site, the various functions were interwoven into an architecturally rich building complex.

The minaret, capped with a ribbed dome that was once covered with green faience tiles, is located on the south side of the building. The first tier is square and trimmed with rows of stalactites, or **muqarna**s vaulting, while the second is cylindrical. The elegant façade has an imposing arched entrance that projects into the street. The doorway is set back in a marble recess covered with a hood of stalactites. A block of pharaonic stone engraved with hieroglyphics was used for the doorsill.

Baffled corridors lead from the entrance, allowing calm sanctuary and privacy from the noisy and dusty Gamaliya Street. To the left is the tomb, its tall dome undecorated except for the small colored glass lights above. The various parts of the building are clearly defined within the irregularly shaped area. On either side of the prayer area are cells for the Sufi scholars. Outside, the imposing portal adjacent to the **khanqah** to the north is the **Hosh Utay (16)**. This is all that remains of a large commercial center that was built in 1817.

Turn and walk back along al-Gamaliya Street past the Sabil–Kuttab and Wikala of Oda Bashi (see 12 above) and beyond to the **Mosque of Mahmud Muharram (17)**, on the corner with Darb al-Masmat. Dating from 1792, this is a good example of a late Ottoman mosque built over shops. It has a simple square room with four central columns supporting a north-facing **malqaf** to catch the breeze and provide light.

At the next corner down al-Gamaliya Street is the irregular site of the seventeenth-century **Ottoman Mosque of Marzuq al-Ahmadi (18)**. Enter the bland narrow lane behind the mosque, Qasr al-Shawq Street, then bear left into Darb al-Tablawi, until you reach the entrance to the **Musafirkhana Palace (19)**. This Ottoman residence was built between 1779 and 1788 but was recently gutted by a fire. The house was originally

POLO PLAYERS

Polo is one of the oldest equestrian sports. At first it was a training game for cavalry units or elite troops. Tribesmen often played it with as many as one hundred to a side, reminiscent of a miniature battle. The game is believed to have originated in Persia (now Iran) and spread to Arabia, then to Tibet. The name of the game is derived from the Tibetan *pulu*, meaning willow, the wood from which the mallets and balls used in the game are made. Polo was introduced into India by Muslim conquerors in the thirteenth century, and then spread to Europe and other parts of the world.

KHANQAHS FOR SUFIS

Sufis took their name from the Arabic word for the coarse woolen garment they wore. Their interpretation of Islam developed from a combination of mysticism and austere self-discipline, though not necessarily celibacy. Sufi orders were not inherently communal until the Sunni revival in the twelfth century in Syria. In Egypt, Salah al-Din endowed the first *khanqah* for Sufis in 1173. The Mamluks made provision for Sufis in *khanqah*s, which were subject to state control, preventing the mystical brotherhoods from becoming politically active. The *khanqah* was essentially a place to study the Quran without the intellectual pretensions of a great *madrasa*.

Outside the Ottoman Mosque of
Marzuq al-Ahmadi, the street is not
just a thoroughfare but also a living
room, a dining area, and a kitchen,
where black-clad old ladies are often
surrounded by pots and pans.

built by Mahmud Muharram, a successful merchant who was also responsible for the mosque bearing his name (see 17 above). His house was the center of an important social group that made the neighborhood fashionable. He died of sunstroke after returning from the **hajj**, the pilgrimage to Mecca. The building's importance increased when, at the beginning of the nineteenth century, Muhammad 'Ali bought it and used it as a royal guest house. In 1830, in a room above the dining room, the future khedive Isma'il was born.

This house was lavishly decorated in the Turkish style. Inside the entrance on the left was the palace's well and water system. Water was transported to the rest of the house through a small aqueduct. From the planted courtyard with its central fountain and large **mashrabiya** panes, entrances led to various parts of the palace. The **salamlik qa'a** had a fine carved ceiling, while the **haramlik qa'a** is decorated in marble panels. Until recently, the palace was restored and used as studios for artists to display their work.

Walk back to al-Gamaliya Street, then northward to al-Qaffasin Street, the next narrow turn to the left, and follow it around to the **Madrasa and Mausoleum of Tatar al-Higaziya (20)**. Here is the tomb of the princess Tatar, the daughter of Sultan al-Nasir Mohammad, who died of the plague in 1360. It is located under a dome at the corner of the two streets and can be seen through an open window where women seek blessings from the princess.

Continue along the short, narrow street until you arrive at the small Bayt al-Qadi Square. This was the former garden of the Mamluk palace of the amir Sayf al-Din Mamay ibn Shadad, a commander under Sultan Qaytbay. On the south end of the square is a building with a five-arched arcade, which is part of the fascinating southern area of the palace, the **Maq'ad of Mamay al-Sayfi (21)**, built in 1496. During the Ottoman period, this loggia was the seat of the court, hence the

Along the short, narrow street leading to Bayt al-Qadi Square is the Mosque, Madrasa, and Mausoleum of Tatar al-Higaziya, containing the tomb of the daughter of Sultan al-Nasir Muhammad.

The *iwan* (one of four vaulted spaces
surrounding the central courtyard of the
Madrasa of Amir Mithqal) provides
a serene place for the faithful to meet
and pray.

MAMLUK *MUQARNAS*

During the Mamluk period, stone was
used to make a variety of decorations. In
particular, the Mamluks were attracted to
the *muqarnas*, a decorative vaulting style
that came to Egypt via Syria. As a result
of an overhang, *muqarnas* gives the
appearance of dripping stalactites,
providing a constant sloping of
corbels that seemed to defy
gravity. By the late Mamluk
period, *muqarnas* had
become very elaborate, and
was used over entrances,
on the balconies of
minarets, around the
tops of walls, and inside
domes. During the
Ottoman period, the use
of stalactites declined.

name of the square. (Bayt al-qadi means 'house of the judge.') The arched
gateway to the southeast of the square is similarly named. Today, part of the
loggia is used as a mosque, and a wall has been erected in front for privacy.

Staying on the north side of the square, follow the street on to the
northwest corner, marked Harat al-Qirmiz. At the end of the street is a short
tunnel-vaulted alley that passes under the 'suspended' **Madrasa of Amir
Mithqal (22)**, built in 1363. This is a cruciform mosque–madrasa, elegantly
raised above the street level, endowed by Sabiq al-Din Mithqal at the height of
his career. He was the chief eunuch at the court of Sultan Muhammad II. The
madrasa, located near his house, was built for teaching Sufi rights. The
entrance is up the steps and through a stalactite-covered portal. Inside, the
sahn (the central courtyard of the mosque), the walls, and the floor are

paneled with colored marble. The four **iwans**, vaulted spaces surrounding the central courtyard, have pointed arches, and two are unusually divided by mezzanine floors and screened with **mashrabiyas**. There is an impressive frieze with Quranic inscriptions and an inlaid **mihrab**, the niche in the wall indicating the direction of Mecca.

Continue west along the winding Darb al-Qirmiz, toward al-Mu'izz Street. On the north side you will see the small **Tomb of Shaykh Sinan (23)**, built in 1585. It gives an indication of the original level of the street during the sixteenth century, when it was two meters lower.

On the left at the junction of al-Mu'izz Street and Darb al-Qirmiz is the **Palace of Amir Bashtak (24)**. This building is a rare example of fourteenth-century domestic architecture in Cairo. The palace was originally five stories high and renowned throughout the city. Today the building has only two floors and a plain façade decorated with **mashrabiya** windows. The amir took advantage of the building's location on al-Mu'izz Street, the main commercial thoroughfare, and rented shops to augment his income.

Access to the palace is from Darb al-Qirmiz, through a courtyard with a bent entrance that ensures privacy. Service areas are on the ground floor, with living and sleeping areas above. The upper floor can be reached through a modern entrance that leads to a large **qa'a**. With its extravagant

The Palace of Amir Bashtak (once five stories high) on al-Mu'izz Street is a rare example of a fourteenth-century domestic building in Cairo.

THE AMIR BASHTAK

Bashtak, who married the daughter of Sultan al-Nasir Muhammad, was one of the most powerful amirs of his time, the other being Amir Qawsun, with whom he had a longstanding feud. He bought the site of his house in 1335 when it still contained remnants of the eastern Fatimid palace. The fact that he acquired such a prominent location is an indication of his wealth and powerful influence. The palace he built was a glittering affair, with guests entertained by musicians and dancing girls.

Unfortunately, the amir Qawsun had Bashtak arrested and executed, while seizing all his possessions.

marble floor and gilded ceiling, this grand reception hall gives some indication of the scale of the original building. In the center of the room stood an elaborate fountain inlaid with colored marble in geometric patterns. Mashrabiya screens along the galleries allowed the women of the house to look on the male guests below without being seen. Lattice windows also provided a way for women to see out onto the busy al-Mu'izz Street below. The direct contrast between the extravagance of the interior and the plain façade of the exterior expresses a sense of discreet privacy.

Upon leaving the Bashtak Palace and entering al-Mu'izz Street, the elegant **Sabil–Kuttab of 'Abd al-Rahman Katkhuda (25)** is prominently placed at the thin wedge end of a block separating the main thoroughfare into two branches. Built in 1764, it fully exploits its location at the street junction. The key for this monument is with the custodian at Bashtak Palace.

The lofty two-story stone structure features a timber balcony screen that is open on three sides. The building extends vertically with its high walls and bronze grilles and is framed by large double arches and delicate columns at the corners. The building is entered from the side street through a stalactite-covered portal. Inside, the **sabil** is faced with tiles imported from Syria, some of them showing a representation of the Ka'ba in Mecca. On the next floor is the **kuttab**, with its carved timber loggia placed on decorated corbels. The overall effect of lightness is provided by an overhanging wooden roof and an elegantly carved ceiling supported by decorated stone columns. While retaining many Mamluk features, this **sabil–kuttab** also reveals Ottoman influences, such as the interlocking inlay patterns on the stone façade and the realistic floral patterns, which were popular in Turkey in the seventeenth century. From the balcony of the **kuttab** is a clear view of the next group of monuments to be visited, Bayn al-Qasrayn ('between the two palaces').

As the site of the royal palaces, Bayn al-Qasrayn was the heart of the Fatimid city. During the Ayyubid and Mamluk periods, the palaces were replaced by other major buildings, particularly the developing structure of the **madrasa**–mosque with the founder's mausoleum attached. Due to the proximity of the Khan al-Khalili bazaar and the busy al-Azhar Road to the south, this cluster of monuments is the most frequented tourist attraction in the area. With its unique architectural character, it represents one of the most important showcases in the historic city. On the west side of al-Mu'izz Street

The elegant Sabil-Kuttab of 'Abd al-Rahman Katkhuda is prominently located in the middle of al-Mu'izz Street and provides fine views of the surroundings from the first-floor terrace.

AMIR 'ABD AL-RAHMAN KATKHUDA

Amir 'Abd al-Rahman Katkhuda was a senior officer of a powerful regiment of Mamluks, the Qazdughli. At one time he was the most influential man in Egypt, although he was more interested in aesthetics than in political ambitions. He became a great patron of the arts, and in his lifetime, he restored or built more than thirty-three buildings and almost doubled the area of al-Azhar mosque. He was later banished to the Holy Cities in Arabia following false charges made by a ruthless Mamluk, 'Ali Bey al-Ghazzawi, who had a grudge against him. He returned to Cairo a sick man and died in 1777.

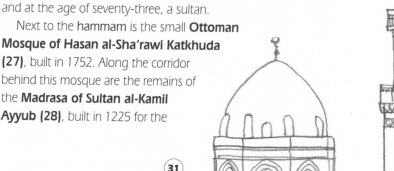

(the site of the western palace), a sequence of spectacular façades 185 meters long developed over a period of one hundred and fifty years. Built by one generation after another, these monuments stand side by side with considerable difference in height, silhouette, shape, and detail, yet they fuse into a single coherent architectural presence, without sacrificing the individual character of any of the buildings.

Part of this area consists of less significant buildings in the sequence, which are nevertheless important in the development of the street as a whole. Walking south along al-Mu'izz Street, a few paces after the Sabil–Kuttab of 'Abd al-Rahman Katkhuda on the west side is the entrance to the **Hammam of Sultan Inal (26)**, built in 1456 and now called simply Hammam Sultan. This public bath is still in use and has been incorporated into a modern building. Inside are large marble reclining slabs and a domed steam room. It was once part of an extensive palace built by Inal, one of Barquq's Mamluks who became an amir then chief of the armies, and at the age of seventy-three, a sultan.

Next to the **hammam** is the small **Ottoman Mosque of Hasan al-Sha'rawi Katkhuda (27)**, built in 1752. Along the corridor behind this mosque are the remains of the **Madrasa of Sultan al-Kamil Ayyub (28)**, built in 1225 for the

study of the Hadith (the sayings of the Prophet). It was the first college built for this purpose in Cairo and became the most respected center in all of Egypt. Sultan al-Kamil Ayyub, the nephew of Salah al-Din, was a generous leader who received St. Francis of Assisi in 1219. All that remains of the **madrasa** are two of the **iwan**s.

Adjoining this ruin is the impressive **Madrasa and Khanqah of Sultan al-Zahir Barquq (29)**. This complex was built between 1384 and 1386 by the architect Ahmad ibn al-Tuluni, Barquq's father-in-law. It was planned as a cruciform **madrasa** to teach the four schools of law, along with accommodation for 125 students, a **khanqah** for sixty Sufis, and a mausoleum for Sultan Barquq. The **madrasa** was also used as a mosque. The bent entrance leads through a passage to the courtyard with a graceful ablution fountain in the center. Access to the four schools is at the corners of the courtyard, through doors decorated with a bronze pattern like that found in carpets.

The decorated ceiling of the arcade along the **qibla** wall is supported by four columns of pharaonic origin. Enameled lamps that are now in

One of the most important showcases in the historic city, built over a period of 150 years
(after *Ecole d'Architecture de Versailles*)

26 *Hammam* of Sultan Inal
27 Mosque of Hasan al-Sha'rawi Katkhuda
28 *Madrasa* of Sultan al-Kamil Ayyub
29 *Madrasa* and *Khanqah* of Sultan al-Zahir Barquq
30 *Madrasa* and Mausoleum of al-Nasir Muhammad ibn Qalawun
31 *Madrasa*, Mausoleum, and *Maristan* of Sultan al-Mansur Qalawun

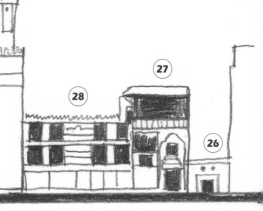

the Islamic Museum used to be suspended by chains from above. There is also a timber **dikka** (a raised platform used for Quranic recitations) and a finely carved **minbar**, or pulpit. The entrance to the domed and highly decorated mausoleum is through a door in the courtyard to the left of the **qibla**. Here, on a marble floor, Barquq's daughter Fatima is buried in sumptuous splendor under gilded stalactites and bands of arabesque inscriptions around the walls. Barquq's body was transfered to a **madrasa** in the northern cemetery built by his son Farag.

Outside, the tall façade is divided into six shallow recesses, each headed with stalactites; the section corresponding to the tomb has lower and upper windows. A band of inscriptions runs along the top of the wall. The arched entrance with stalactites above features bronze-plated double doors inlaid with silver. In the nineteenth century, the original dome collapsed and was replaced with the present structure in 1893. The elegant minaret is formed of three octagonal tiers covered with bold carvings. The sultan was so pleased with the results that he gave each of the workmen two gold pieces.

The next building, set back from the façade of Barquq's complex, is the **Madrasa and Mausoleum of al-Nasir Muhammad ibn Qalawun (30)**. Sultan al-Nasir ('the victorious'), one of Sultan Qalawun's five sons, was a small man of ruthless courage and great intellect whose reign marked a high point in Mamluk culture. Some thirty surviving mosques were built during his time. This complex was begun in 1295 by the Mongol sultan Kitbugha, who ruled only briefly, and was completed by al-Nasir in 1304, about eighty years after Barquq's monument next door.

The white marble Gothic doorway came from the Crusader church of St. George in Acre, which was captured by al-Nasir's older brother. At the apex of the pointed arch the word 'Allah' has been added. This portal leads into a passage separating the mausoleum from the **madrasa**, which are entered by two doors at the far end. The tomb is on the right, and the **madrasa**, the first in Cairo to use the cruciform plan, is to the left of the entrance. Inside, the four **iwan**s once contained the four different law schools. On the east side is a fine stucco **mihrab**. Now the interior is in poor condition, however, with only traces of its lavish decorations surviving. The mausoleum contains the bodies of al-Nasir's mother and son. The sultan was buried in the adjoining mausoleum built by his father, Sultan Qalawun.

The white marble Gothic doorway of the Madrasa and Mausoleum of al-Nasir Muhammad Ibn Qalawun came from the Crusader church of St George in Acre.

The narrow façade consists of the entrance, over which the minaret sits, and the **madrasa** and the tomb on either side. The elevation shows tall windows and a band of continuous script, originally gilded all the way across to commemorate Sultan al-Nasir. The first of the three tiers of the minaret is covered with an exquisitely carved stucco surface, probably of North African workmanship, that gives a lace-like effect. Little decoration remains on the back and sides, however. The second tier was added some hundred years later, and the third is Ottoman.

The last of the group of buildings in the sequence is the earliest and most outstanding example of the monumental complexes of the Mamluks, **the Madrasa, Mausoleum, and Maristan of Sultan al-Mansur Qalawun (31)**. These three buildings were planned along an imposing corridor five meters wide and ten meters high. On the left is the formal entrance to the courtyard of the **madrasa**, through a bronze door in a round arch. The present entrance, however, is through a dilapidated window opening. On the right is Qalawun's well-preserved mausoleum. At the end of the corridor was the **maristan** (Persian for 'place of illness,' or hospital), now destroyed and its entrance blocked. Only three of the arched bays remain at the rear.

Although the **madrasa** is in a poor state, there are strong indications of its former splendor. The east **iwan** is highly decorated, and its layout is reminiscent of a Byzantine church, with three aisles, classical columns, and a double-tiered arch above. The well-preserved mausoleum is overwhelmingly beautiful. It has an octagonal floor plan but a square interior space supported by red granite columns from the pharaonic era with gilded capitals. The entire room is richly decorated with marble strips, panels of colored stone, and attractive stuccowork. A point that becomes clear in the window ledge is that the discrepancy between the street elevation and the internal orientation toward Mecca was resolved by thickening the walls accordingly.

The cenotaph, screened by **mashrabiya**s, contains the bodies of Qalawun and a number of his sons, including al-Nasir. The ornamental **qibla** is seven meters high. The original dome was demolished by 'Abd al-Rahman Katkhuda and a new one built in 1903. Over the centuries, the tomb became the site for special ceremonies and celebrations.

SULTAN AL-MANSUR QALAWUN

Qalawun (whose name means 'duck') was a Turk from the region around the lower Volga ruled by the Golden Horde. He was proud that Sultan Ayyub paid one thousand dinars for him. He became sultan in 1279 and founded a dynasty that lasted almost one hundred years. After being treated at Nur al-Din's hospital in Damascus, he included in his building complex the *maristan*, which functioned as a charity hospital and a center for the study of medicine. This building continued to be used as a medical center until Muhammad 'Ali introduced modern hospitals in the nineteenth century. Qalawun died of a fever in 1290, on his way to Acre to fight the Crusaders.

SULTAN AL-ZAHIR BARQUQ

Barquq (whose name in Arabic means 'plum') was one of the first slaves to be imported into Cairo from the Caucasus, between the Black and the Caspian seas. Lodged in the Citadel, these slaves were known as Burgi Mamluks. Barquq was purchased and educated by the amir Yalbugha al-'Umari. Later he was freed, and after a series of intrigues, he seized power in 1382. He consolidated his position by marrying the widow of the sultan Sha'ban. He filled many important military posts with Circassians. Consequently, the period of his and his sons' rule is known as that of the Circassian Mamluks.

The hospital was remarkable for its time. It was open to all, with services free of charge. Even musicians and storytellers were provided to soothe the patients. There has been some kind of hospital on this site for the last seven hundred years; today, it is a modern eye hospital.

From al-Mu'izz Street, only the façades of the **madrasa** and mausoleum are visible. The distribution of the bay windows gives the impression of a three-story building. Above the first tier of windows runs an inscription in stone across the façade. Remarkably, the entire complex was completed in thirteen months, in the years 1284–85.

The imposing minaret is a square stone shaft crowned with a balcony of stalactites, topped with a second, smaller tier. The third and final tier is round and made of bricks and decorated with stucco. It is a replacement built by al-Nasir after damage from the 1302 earthquake. On the north end of the façade, a **sabil**, the earliest in Cairo, was added in 1346 by Amir Arghun al-Ala'i.

As you come out of Qalawun's complex, glance back to the other side of the street at the charming **Sabil–Kuttab of Isma'il Pasha (32)** opposite al-Nasir's **madrasa**, which commemorates the expedition to Sudan by Muhammad

ENDOWMENTS

A mausoleum on its own is not regarded as being religious in Egypt. To preserve his tomb for posterity, an amir would add one or more religious buildings on the same site, such as a *madrasa, khanqah,* or *sabil–kuttab*. By building religious institutions from his own revenues, he could then endow lands from his estate for upkeep and running expenses of the institutions after his death. A *waqf*, or endowment deed, was used to cover all expenses, including that of his tomb. Now more than ninety-five percent of the monuments in the historic city are owned by the Ministry of Waqfs. As a result of rent controls, revenues are inadequate, and the monuments have become dilapidated.

The delicately rounded façade of the imposing Sabil of Isma'il Pasha was built by Muhammad Ali for his son in 1822. This view is from the doorway of al-Nasir's complex.

'Ali's son Isma'il. A cruel and callous man, he was burned alive with his officers in 1822. This building with a rounded front was built by Muhammad 'Ali in 1828. The kuttab was located in rooms on either side of the sabil. Above the windows can be seen the official seal of Sultan Mahmud II.

The house of 'Uthman Katkhuda, an unassuming building from its street entrance, contains a large qa'a some seventeen meters high and is a good example of eighteenth-century domestic architecture in Cairo.

TREE OF PEARLS

Her name was Shagarat al-Durr, meaning 'tree of pearls.' She was an Armenian slave chosen by al-Salih Nagm al-Din Ayyub as his second wife. Ayyub became sultan in 1240 and later died fighting the Crusaders in the Delta. Tree of Pearls kept his death a secret until his son Turan Shah returned to Cairo. When Turan was murdered, she seized power and became sultana. For the first time since Cleopatra, a woman ruled Egypt, if only for eighty days. Her reign marked a period of political transition, from the royal dynasty of the Ayyubids to the dominance of the Mamluks, among them Qalawun, al-Nasir, and Barquq.

Opposite Qalawun's mausoleum is Bayt al-Qadi Street, leading back to the small square (see 21 above). Here are numerous shops selling a variety of scales and weights. Halfway up the street on the left-hand side are the remains of a large house built in 1350. It is best known as the eighteenth-century **House of 'Uthman Katkhuda (33)**, the father of 'Abd al-Rahman Katkhuda, the governor of Cairo from 1730 to 1736. A long passage leads into a large qa'a some seventeen meters high in the center. On the roof is a good example of a large malqaf designed to distribute the breeze through the house.

The buildings opposite Qalawun's complex on al-Mu'izz Street are part of the **Madrasa and Mausoleum of al-Salih Nagm al-Din Ayyub (34)**. The madrasa was built in 1242 as two parallel blocks,

each housing two of the four Sunni legal rites, bisected by a narrow street and crowned with the minaret over a richly decorated doorway. This was the first **madrasa** to be built in Egypt, incorporating all four of the schools of law. The mausoleum north of the **madrasa** was built by Ayyub's wife, Shagarat al-Durr, who laid her husband's body to rest in 1250 with elaborate ceremonies and much public grief. Adjacent to the mausoleum on the north side was the **madrasa** of Sultan Baybars I, of which only one bay survives, used as a store. The combination of these two types of buildings (**madrasa** and mausoleum) later became the standard Mamluk architectural formula. With the importance of the four schools of law, however, this complex developed into more than a center for worship and learning: it became the state tribunal.

Across the street from the Qalawun complex is the restored Mausoleum of al-Salih Nagm al-Din Ayyub, well worth a visit.

The clutter of pots and pans of all shapes and sizes can be seen along the coppersmith's market, dominated by the minaret of the Madrasa and Mausoleum of al-Salih Nagm al-Din Ayyub.

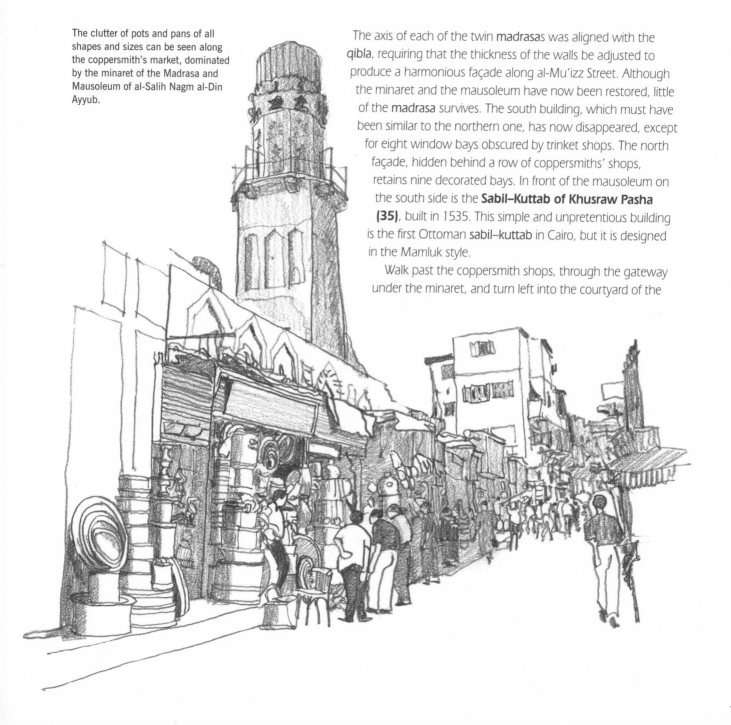

The axis of each of the twin **madrasa**s was aligned with the qibla, requiring that the thickness of the walls be adjusted to produce a harmonious façade along al-Mu'izz Street. Although the minaret and the mausoleum have now been restored, little of the **madrasa** survives. The south building, which must have been similar to the northern one, has now disappeared, except for eight window bays obscured by trinket shops. The north façade, hidden behind a row of coppersmiths' shops, retains nine decorated bays. In front of the mausoleum on the south side is the **Sabil–Kuttab of Khusraw Pasha (35)**, built in 1535. This simple and unpretentious building is the first Ottoman sabil–kuttab in Cairo, but it is designed in the Mamluk style.

Walk past the coppersmith shops, through the gateway under the minaret, and turn left into the courtyard of the

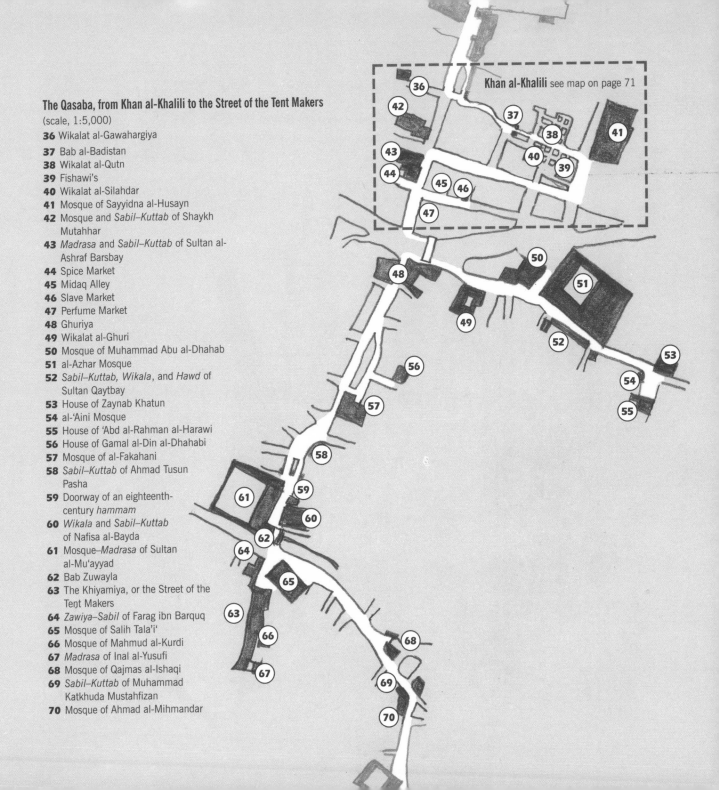

The Qasaba, from Khan al-Khalili to the Street of the Tent Makers

(scale, 1:5,000)

36 Wikalat al-Gawahargiya
37 Bab al-Badistan
38 Wikalat al-Qutn
39 Fishawi's
40 Wikalat al-Silahdar
41 Mosque of Sayyidna al-Husayn
42 Mosque and *Sabil–Kuttab* of Shaykh Mutahhar
43 *Madrasa* and *Sabil–Kuttab* of Sultan al-Ashraf Barsbay
44 Spice Market
45 Midaq Alley
46 Slave Market
47 Perfume Market
48 Ghuriya
49 Wikalat al-Ghuri
50 Mosque of Muhammad Abu al-Dhahab
51 al-Azhar Mosque
52 *Sabil–Kuttab*, *Wikala*, and *Hawd* of Sultan Qaytbay
53 House of Zaynab Khatun
54 al-'Aini Mosque
55 House of 'Abd al-Rahman al-Harawi
56 House of Gamal al-Din al-Dhahabi
57 Mosque of al-Fakahani
58 *Sabil–Kuttab* of Ahmad Tusun Pasha
59 Doorway of an eighteenth-century *hammam*
60 *Wikala* and *Sabil–Kuttab* of Nafisa al-Bayda
61 Mosque–*Madrasa* of Sultan al-Mu'ayyad
62 Bab Zuwayla
63 The Khiyamiya, or the Street of the Tent Makers
64 *Zawiya–Sabil* of Farag ibn Barquq
65 Mosque of Salih Tala'i'
66 Mosque of Mahmud al-Kurdi
67 *Madrasa* of Inal al-Yusufi
68 Mosque of Qajmas al-Ishaqi
69 *Sabil–Kuttab* of Muhammad Katkhuda Mustahfizan
70 Mosque of Ahmad al-Mihmandar

Khan al-Khalili see map on page 71

To the left of Bab al-Badistan, the gate attributed to Sultan al-Ghuri, is the Naguib Mahfouz café, named after Egypt's famous writer. It is a convenient place to stop and rest in this predominantly tourist area.

northern part of the al-Salih **madrasa**. One arched **iwan** still stands and is now a prayer area. On the east side are remnants of the other **iwan**. A stairway inside the minaret leads to the balcony of the shaft, which gives excellent views of the surrounding buildings.

Following the line of shops past the **sabil–kuttab** and the pots and pans of the coppersmiths' market, continue along al-Mu'izz Street into the gold market, with its flashy window displays. The short passage with a massive gate on the right leads to a cluster of Ottoman monuments: first, the **Wikalat al-Gawahargiya (36)**, then beyond to the **wikala** and **sabil–kuttab** of Gamal al-Din al-Dhahabi, an important gold merchant, and also to the mosque of Taghri Bardi.

On the left side of al-Mu'izz Street is the narrow lane of Sikkat al-Badistan, which leads into Khan al-Khalili. This is the bazaar that entices both Egyptian and foreign visitors to shop and bargain for a variety of trinkets in gold, silver, leather, glass, wood, and stone, in more than a thousand premises. Turn here and continue walking east until you reach the sixteenth-century **Bab al-Badistan (37)**, attributed to Sultan al-

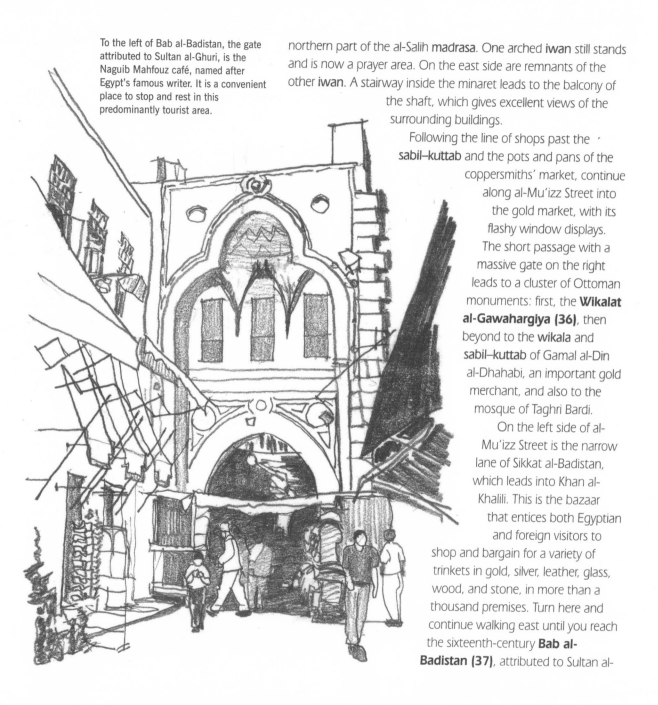

Ghuri. Just before this gate is the Naguib Mahfouz Café, named after Egypt's famous writer. It is a good place to stop to rest and contemplate the significance of this lively area. It also has one of the cleanest toilets in historic Cairo. In the evening, there is live music and fortune-telling to arouse your curiosity.

This area was once the cemetery of the Fatimid elite, but the tombs were removed and placed outside the city by Salah al-Din. The origins of the lively bazaar go back to 1384, when one of Sultan Barquq's amirs, Jarkas al-Khalili, built a large **khan** providing accommodation for merchants and their trades.

The **khan** was three stories high and became the most successful mercantile building in the area, selling spices, porcelain, precious stones, and fine cloths from the east. It soon attracted other merchants, food sellers, and water carriers, and numerous small shops spread out into the neighboring streets.

In 1511, Sultan al-Ghuri demolished the **khan** and on the same site erected a new imposing **wikala** bearing his name. This is the now dilapidated **Wikalat al-Qutn (38)**, once a commercial center for cotton. Other **wikala**s were built nearby, making this area a well-established commercial center. Although it declined under the Ottomans, it flourished again during Muhammad 'Ali's rule. Today, Khan al-Khalili is a warren of small factories and shops displaying often tacky and sometimes exotic oriental goods.

Fishawi's is probably the most interesting café in the Khan al-Khalili, with its large mirrors and small coffee tables. It was once the meeting point for artists and literati, including Naguib Mahfouz.

Shopping in the vibrant Khan al-Khalili is a lively activity, and it is possible to find almost anything you are looking for in the bazaar. If something you require is not already for sale, you can have it made. Recommended shops with a variety of products are shown on the map. A number of places for eating and drinking (non-alcoholic) are recommended, in addition to the elegant Khan al-Khalili Restaurant adjoining the Naguib Mahfouz Café. Such places include Egyptian Pancakes, where you can watch the paper-thin dough being spun, or, for a sit-down meal, al-Halwagi Restaurant (both on the short al-Bustan al-Suq al-Fatimi Street). For a clean and unpretentious meal (but not for vegetarians), try kufta and kabab at al-Dahhan Restaurant

Built on the site of the cemetery of the Fatimid caliphs, the Mosque of Sayyidna al-Husayn is one of the busiest mosques in Cairo, although inaccessible to non-Muslims.

on Muski Street. A good view of the city can be had from the terrace café in al-Husayn Hotel, though the place is now only a pale shadow of its former glory.

The most interesting coffee house, however, is **Fishawi's (39)**, now much reduced by redevelopment. In its heyday, it was frequented by artists and literati. One of its regulars was the author Naguib Mahfouz. Here you can order fresh mint tea or Turkish coffee and enjoy a waterpipe.

Once you have rested at the Naguib Mahfouz Café, continue along Sikkat al-Badistan until you reach the alley of Sikkat al-Qabwa, opposite the entrance to Wikalat al-Qutn, where al-Ghuri's decorated Bab al-Badistan stands. Through this gate are a number of **wikala**s, including **Wikalat al-Silahdar (40)**. Continue to the end of Sikkat al-Badistan through the area of shops and apartment blocks, which were built in 1936 in a neo-Islamic style. At the end of this narrow street is Husayn Square, the forecourt to the large mosque of the same name.

The present **Mosque of Sayyidna al-Husayn (41)** was built in the late nineteenth century on the site of the cemetery of the Fatimid caliphs. This is the principal mosque in Cairo and some ten thousand people may visit daily to pray. The mosque is not accessible to non-Muslims. Here also is the tomb of Husayn, one of the sons of Caliph 'Ali, grandson of the Prophet, which has been rebuilt and restored several times. On the southeast side of the mosque is the mausoleum said to contain the head of al-Husayn (the rest of his body is reputed to be in Iraq). The ten-day-long festival commemorating al-Husayn's birth is one of the most important events in the Muslim calender and attracts thousands of people from all over the rural Delta. Pilgrims stay wherever they can: in parks, on verges, and in many of the

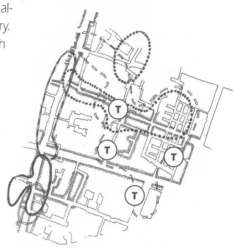

Khan al-Khalili, the tourist market area
(scale, 1:5,000)

T Toilets

•••• Jewelry
▬▬ Gold
▫ ▫ Main bazaar
▬▬ Spice
═══ Perfume

monuments. Dazzling colored lights are strung around stalls offering food, goods, and amusement.

The street parallel to Sikkat al-Badistan to the south is al-Muski Street, first cut through the historic city by Muhammad 'Ali, then extended by Isma'il. Now it has lost its upper-class pretensions and has been absorbed into the modest standards of Khan al-Khalili.

Walk back west along al-Muski Street to the junction with al-Mu'izz Street. On the northwest corner is the **Mosque and Sabil–Kuttab of Shaykh Mutahhar (42)**, erected in 1744. The mosque was built next to an existing sabil–kuttab provided by 'Abd al-Rahman Katkhuda (see also 25 above). On the southwest corner is the imposing **Madrasa and Sabil–Kuttab of Sultan al-Ashraf Barsbay**

(43), built in 1425. It is cruciform in plan, with a mausoleum attached on the street façade. The sabil–kuttab is near the portal entrance at the south end. A three-tiered decorated minaret crowned by an onion-shaped dome marks the entrance to the building. A long, bent corridor connects the street with the courtyard. On the left, along the corridor, an alcove with a **mashrabiya** screen contains the cistern that supplies the **sabil**. The mausoleum is a tall, square room in the east corner of the building, with a window overlooking the street. In the center of the domed room are two marble cenotaphs, where the wife and son of the sultan are buried. Barsbay himself is buried in the northern cemetery. The inscription around the **iwan**s is an ironic reminder as to how reserved funds should be spent for the maintenance of the monument.

Coming out of the **madrasa**, turn right into al-Mu'izz Street again and you are in the **Spice Market (44)**. This part of al-Mu'izz Street, and Harat Hamzawi, the lane to the south of Barsbay's **madrasa**, display sacks heaped full of brightly-colored powders, seeds, cloves, and nuts. The market's location is no accident: Sultan Barsbay, whose **madrasa** dominates the area, monopolized the trade and used the profits to subsidize his foreign campaigns and erect many of his prestigious buildings.

The next street after al-Muski along al-Mu'izz Street is the narrow al-Sanadiya Street. A little way up on the left is **Midaq**

BARGAINING

Shops selling particular products are clustered together, encouraging comparative bargaining, which is expected in most shops. Your first offer should be about two-thirds the asking price. You may then end up somewhere between the trader's price and yours. If his price is too high, try another shop. If it is too low, this may be due to inferior quality, so check with other shops in the area. Once you agree to a price, however, it is considered bad manners to change your mind about a purchase. Tea or a soft drink is often offered as a sign of hospitality when contemplating an expensive purchase, and can be accepted with no further obligations.

On the northwest corner of al-Muski Street along al-Mu'izz Street is the Mosque and Sabil-Kuttab of Shaykh Mutahhar, and on the southwest corner is the Madrasa and Sabil-Kuttab of Sultan al-Ashraf Barsbay *(after l'École d'Architecture de Versailles)*.

Alley (45), the setting of Naguib Mahfouz's famous novel of the same name. His masterpiece of accurate character portrayal offers a fascinating insight into an Egyptian society that is now past. A little further along Haradiya Street is the dilapidated façade of Wikalat al-Galaba, built in the early sixteenth century. This was the site of Cairo's infamous **Slave Market (46)**. Galaba means 'foreign slaves.' Like any other commodity, slaves were stored in warehouses by merchants until they were purchased.

Walk back to al-Mu'izz Street and turn left into the **Perfume Market (47)**, where a profusion of shops sell local blends as well as imitations of well-

Built in 1927, al-Azhar Street cuts the historic city into two parts, with only a metal footbridge to link the historic thoroughfare of al-Mu'izz Street.

known brands. Amidst a myriad of odors, you can buy decorated bottles as well, filled with the perfume of your choice. The shops also sell incense and the famous Kohl, a thick black powder used as eyeliner to lessen the glare from the sun. Kohl has been used by Egyptian women since pharaonic times. The end of the perfume market is marked by the main thoroughfare, al-Azhar Street, that carves the historic city into two parts. This road was built in 1927 and financed by the Tramway Company, while the flyover was completed in 1984. Above ground, a metal footbridge built by the army provides the only link across al-Mu'izz Street, the historic spine of the city, uninterrupted for more than one thousand years.

Descending the steps from the footbridge on the south side, you are confronted by the **Ghuriya (48)**, the imposing Mamluk buildings on either side of al-Mu'izz Street. The complex, a splendid example of Cairene civic design, was built by Sultan Qansuh al-Ghuri. These buildings consist of a mausoleum, a **sabil–kuttab**, and a **maq'ad** on the east side of the street and a **madrasa** on the west. In the eighteenth century, the two buildings were linked by a massive timber roof across al-Mu'izz Street, which created an impressive urban setting. This was the last major Mamluk construction prior to Ottoman occupation.

The square, four-tiered minaret is one of the tallest in the historic city. Its top is crowned with five bulbs, although the original had only four. The three

POWDERS IN MANY COLORS

A wide range of spices are not only essential ingredients in an Egyptian kitchen, but are also promoted by shopkeepers as healing remedies for a variety of ailments, from pneumonia (use *habbit al-baraka*) to impotence (take *nusgha*). They also sell *hinna'*, which is used by Egyptian women to color their hair and paint patterns on the palms of their hands for weddings and other ceremonies. *Karkadeh*, the dried flowers of the hibiscus plant, is made into a delicious drink, taken hot or cold.

THE SLAVE MARKET

Wikalat al-Galaba was the slave market since Mamluk times. Under Napoleon's rule, white slaves were usually sold by contract and included kidnapped adults and children who had been taken in payment of debts. During the nineteenth century, the market dealt in black slaves from Ethiopia, Sudan, and Somalia. It was later removed to an area near the Qaytbay mosque because the slaves were blamed for the spread of diseases. Under pressure from western governments, slavery was abolished in the 1850s, although Circassian, Nubian, and Ethiopian women were still in great demand, thus continuing the trade illegally for much longer.

The Ghuriya, the imposing Mamluk buildings
on either side of al-Mu'izz Street, are seen
from al-Azhar Street, with the metal barrier
separating heavy traffic.

windowed recesses on the al-Mu'izz façade create a distinctive irregular space in the street, along with an enormous arched entrance decorated with stalactites. Sadly, in recent years, this building has taken a battering from well-intentioned but never-ending restoration.

On the other side of the street is the mausoleum with its robust **sabil–kuttab** at the north corner of the building. The dome was rebuilt three times and finally replaced with a flat timber roof in 1869. Through the entrance and up a flight of steps to the right is the tomb. Al-Ghuri was not actually buried in his mausoleum. He died fighting the Ottomans, and his body was never found. To the left is the prayer hall, where spectacular whirling dervish dancers now perform at eight o'clock on Wednesday and Saturday evenings, a spectacle that should not be missed.

Adjoining the mausoleum is the enclosed **maq'ad** overlooking a courtyard. It can be entered from al-Azhar Road, through the first entrance, now below street level. The building was intended for the Sufis to hold their meetings, but the complex lacks accommodation, although a few living units are provided in the **madrasa**.

Below the covered area in al-Mu'izz Street was the silk market. Today the silk merchants, along with the roof, have gone, but textiles are still in colorful abundance.

Wikalat al-Ghuri, currently used as a cultural center, has an imposing façade.

After the entrance to the **maq'ad**, continue about a hundred meters along Tablita Street to the **Wikalat al-Ghuri (49)**. Here, merchants kept their animals on the ground floor and lived on the first floor. The remaining stories above were rented as dwellings. The uniform windows of the external façade, with the top row screened by large **mashrabiya** panels, are as impressive as any renaissance palace in Italy. A tall decorated portal leads into the courtyard. Here the pattern of elevations echoes the exterior, with the addition of arcades and a gallery on the first floor. The building's current use as cultural center

SULTAN QANSUH AL-GHURI

Qansuh al-Ghuri was the forty-sixth
Mamluk sultan and the last of any
influence before the Ottomans arrived.
When Sultan Tumanbay was deposed,
the young Mamluks chose him as their
new leader. He accepted the sultanate,
but only reluctantly, at the age of sixty
and ruled for fifteen years, a long time by
Mamluk standards. At the age of seventy-
five, al-Ghuri died fighting the
Ottomans in Syria, and his
body was never found.
Consequently, al-Ghuri is
not buried in the splendid
tomb chamber he built
for himself.

makes it seem tidy and sterile. At the peak of its use as a **wikala**, it would have
been alive with the bustle of bargaining buyers and sellers and energetic
porters unloading exotic merchandise from pack animals.

Tablita Street leads eastward into Zaynab Khatun Street and then onto al-
Azhar Alley and to the edge of the historic city. Running almost parallel to al-
Azhar Road, this stretch crosses behind the university adjacent to the great
mosque, where it has the authentic quality of a medieval street, almost
unchanged by centuries of decay. The numerous historic buildings here are
sadly dilapidated and in dire need of attention. To the south of
the alley is the Batiniya district, once notorious for
drug use, until the police cleaned up the area.

On the corner opposite al-Azhar mosque is
the **Mosque of Muhammad Abu al-
Dhahab (50)**, built by a man who earned
his nickname ('possessor of gold') by

Facing the busy al-Azhar Street is the
Mosque of Muhammad Abu al-Dhahab,
part of a large complex of the last
religious buildings undertaken by
the Mamluks.

The double arched gate entrance to al-Azhar Mosque, called "the Gate of the Barbers," is where students had their heads shaved. Probably the oldest university in the world, the mosque is a microcosm of historic Cairo.

distributing gold coins to the people. The mosque was part of a large complex of the last religious buildings undertaken by the Mamluks, begun in 1774. It contained a **madrasa**, a library, a **takiya** (now used as a store for the university), latrines, and fountains. The dilapidated structures opposite the Tablita fruit and vegetable market are the rear of the **takiya** and the **hawd** (a watering trough for animals). Around the corner, on Gamal Husayn Street, the façade unfolds with its large dome and massive minaret. It clearly benefits from its proximity to al-Azhar Mosque and creates a splendid skyline. At ground level, a group of shops were provided to help with the cost of maintaining the buildings.

On the other side of Gamal Husayn Street is **al-Azhar Mosque (51)**, founded in 970. It is probably the oldest university in the world and still the major theological center in Islam. Scholars from many parts of the Islamic world come here to study the Quran. Today, the structure of al-Azhar is a microcosm of historic Cairo, as many additions have been made by prominent leaders wishing to further embellish the mosque.

To grasp the splendor of this historic mosque, it is best to follow the central axis to the **qibla**

The distinctive architectural features of the Hawd (left) and Sabil-Kuttab (right) of Sultan Qaytbay, often used as focal points for social interaction.

and beyond. The main entrance is on Gamal Husayn, through the double arch of the Ottoman Bab al-Muzayyinin ('gate of the barbers'), where students had their heads shaved. On either side are two Mamluk madrasas: on the left, the Aqbughawiya, topped with a minaret and dating from 1340, and on the right, the Taybarsiya, dating from 1309. The latter contains the most precious manuscripts of the al-Azhar library.

The grand passage leads to the gate of Sultan Qaytbay, which was built in 1469 and its minaret added in 1475. The stone gate is decorated with delicately carved stalactites. Slightly to the west, the large minaret with the double finial was donated by Sultan al-Ghuri. The vast central courtyard is the original from Fatimid times, although decorations were added in the twelfth century.

EMPTY RESTORATIONS

The best way to secure the upkeep of so many historic buildings is to use them appropriately. In Cairo, with few exceptions, restored monuments are usually left empty and with little provision for regular maintenance. They fall into neglect and disrepair quickly. In contrast, mosques that are in constant use are better looked after than other listed buildings. The *wikala* of al-Ghuri, which has been converted for use as cultural center, is one of the few well-preserved buildings in Cairo.

SHAYKHS

A *shaykh* in a crowd can be distinguished by his gray robes and red cap wrapped in a white muslin turban. *Shaykh* is the title given to government officials of al-Azhar and a title of respect for a distinguished scholar, often the head of a Sufi community. The extent of a *shaykh*'s influence usually depended upon his own will and character. The idea of a *shaykh* being a merchant prince is not an Egyptian concept, for spiritual prominence here has never been directly associated with wealth.

The decorative *mashrabiya* casement over the entrance to the House of Gamal al-Din al-Dhahabi.

WALKING

Since open space accounts for less than one percent of the historic city's total area, the streets (accounting for 23 percent) are an important substitute. The crush of people is particularly apparent in the textile market, where pedestrians compete for access with peddlers, carts, and many kinds of vehicles. Those who are not accustomed to walking through such busy thoroughfares may find the experience daunting. Local people have their own way of coping with the situation: they angle one shoulder forward and zigzag quickly to avoid bumping into others. Their eyes usually dart from side to side, anticipating hazards.

Continuing on the same axis is the sanctuary, which is entered through a small domed area. Behind the mihrab are four rows of arcades added by 'Abd al-Rahman Katkhuda. Close by to the right is his tomb and tall minaret, built in 1753. From here Bab al-Sa'ida leads into al-Azhar Alley.

The blank wall to the left of the mosque entrance is al-Azhar University, destined for a new campus location over the next few years. Across the street are the **Sabil–Kuttab, Wikala, and Hawd of Sultan Qaytbay (52)**. Directly opposite the mosque entrance on the right side is the elaborately carved hawd structure, built in 1496 to provide drinking water for animals. On the left is the wikala, built in 1477, of which only the façade remains intact. Similar to the one inside Bab al-Nasr (see 3 above), it once provided a place for animals on the ground floor, with accommodation units above for merchants, travelers, and locals. Attached on the corner is the highly decorated entrance to the sabil–kuttab.

A little further along the alley to the east, the **House of Zaynab Khatun (53)** projects into the street. This is a Mamluk house built around a traditional courtyard for Mithqal-Suduni, a chef to the sultan, in 1468 and refurbished in 1713 with some Ottoman extravagance. The house is named after Zaynab Khatun, the last woman to live there. The building diagonally opposite is **al-'Aini Mosque (54)**, while on the south side of the small garden is the **House of 'Abd al-Rahman al-Harawi (55)**, built in 1731. Both these houses have been restored by the French Government and are regularly used for a wide range of cultural events.

Walk back to al-Mu'izz Street and turn south. Here in the textile market, the foot traffic is noticeably intense. Continue walking until you come to a fork in the road. Bear left and continue on until the next left turning into Harat Khushqadam. About one hundred meters east on this medieval street, on the left-hand side, is the **House of Gamal al-Din al-Dhahabi (56)**, built in 1634. This is a well-preserved example of an Ottoman house built in the Mamluk style. A bent passage gives access to a charming courtyard overlooked by the maq'ad, or loggia, on the south side above the entrance. To the east of the maq'ad is the qa'a, decorated with a high dome and dados of inlaid marble on the walls. Gamal al-Din was a wealthy merchant and chief of the merchants' guild; his wikala still stands behind Wikalat al-Gawahargiya (see also 36 above).

The House of 'Abd al-Rahman al-Harawi
with its unassuming entrance is now used as
a cultural center. The house is adjacent to a
small square, a rare luxury in the densely
packed historic city.

This view of the side entrance to the Mosque of al-Fakahani is from the narrow lane which is heavily used by merchants and tradesmen, from the storage of goods in sacks to a place for shoe-shine boys.

Walk back west along Harat Khushqadam and turn left, where you stand before the side entrance of the **Mosque of al-Fakahani (57)**. The original mosque was built by the Fatimids in 1148, although only the magnificent carved wooden doors remain. The existing mosque (for fruit sellers, as the name implies) was rebuilt in 1735. Standing beyond the mosque further down al-Mu'izz Street is the **Sabil–Kuttab of Ahmad Tusun Pasha (58)**, where the lavishlly decorated timber dome of the **sabil** is framed between the minarets of Bab Zuwayla in the distance. With so much of the city's character still intact, a visitor may stand back to admire one monument and immediately become aware of a link with another.

This **sabil**, built in 1820, is characteristic of the Muhammad 'Ali period and similar in structure to the one opposite the al-Nasir complex along the Bayn al-Qasrayn (see 32 above). The rooms of the **kuttab** (currently used as a primary school) are on either side of the bow-fronted **sabil**. Ahmad Tusun was Muhammad 'Ali's second son, who led campaigns against Saudi Arabia. He died in 1816 after contracting the plague.

Continue walking south after the **sabil** and bear to the left at the next fork. Just before the street widens again is believed to be the location of the first south Fatimid double gate and walls built by Gawhar in 969, prior to the extension of the city by Badr al-Gamali, where the present Bab Zuwayla stands today. On the left, opposite the large mosque, is the discreet doorway of an **Eighteenth-century Hammam (59)** that was still in use until recently. Originally, it was divided into two sections: one for men, accessible by this entrance, and the other (now demolished) for women and children, who entered from the rear. When the **hammam** was built, a **mustawqad** (heating unit) at the rear of the bath was also used for cooking **ful mudammas** (the traditional bean dish), providing breakfast for more than twenty-five thousand people every day. The fuel used was garbage from the surrounding streets (this was the traditional way of disposing of solid waste). Most residents in the immediate vicinity of the **hammam** are still employed in the production of **ful mudammas**, though they now cook with gas.

The buildings adjoining the **hammam** include the **Wikala and Sabil–Kuttab of Nafisa al-Bayda (60)**. The wikala was a commercial center for sugar and nuts, and the area was well known for its sweets and pastries. Dating from 1796, the impressive façade, with its elegant **mashrabiya** windows above the grand entrance, is almost intact, although the building itself is in a dilapidated state. Entered from al-Mu'izz Street, the **wikala** provided storage in vaulted rooms on the ground floor, with accommodation for merchants and visitors above. Additional tenement lodgings for poor people were provided on the upper floors, which were entered from the side street. Today, the **wikala** is mostly occupied by people involved in the production and peddling of **ful mudammas**.

Immediately adjacent to the **wikala** is the charming **sabil–kuttab**, also built in 1796. Its rounded front was the popular style of that period, although the building's combination with such a commercial structure is unusual. The **kuttab**, which was in use until 1958, was quite small, with the usual provision for a teacher's room and a toilet. The façade of this small but elegant structure is finely wrought with detailed wood carvings, marble columns, and limestone walls. An illusion of a three-story building is created through the horizontal divisions of **muqarnas** near ground level, the timber eaves with a carved soffit on the first floor, and an elegant arcaded screen and row of horseshoe arches.

These buildings were provided by Nafisa al-Bayda, a powerful woman with a strong personality who played a leading role between Napoleon's conquering entourage and the disgruntled Mamluk hierarchy. She was believed to have lived over the entrance of the **wikala** in the section with the **mashrabiya**, which was known as al-Qasr, or 'the palace.' Nafisa was the only woman to have a surviving charitable monument on the prestigious al-Mu'izz Street, which shows the extent of her influence.

Adjoining the **sabil–kuttab** is the gate to the quarter behind al-Mu'izz Street. The name of this neighborhood seems to have changed over time, but its medieval name of Hammam (referring

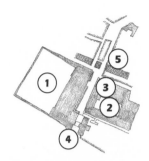

Probable location of the early Fatimid double gate (scale, 1:5,000)

1 Mosque–*Madrasa* of Sultan al-Mu'ayyad
2 *Wikala* and Sabil–Kuttab of Nafisa al-Bayda
3 *Hammam*
4 Bab Zuwayla
5 Presumed site of the early Fatimid double gate

THE *HAMMAM*

Important social occasions in a Muslim's life once centered around the local *hammam*, or public bath, which was located both in the city center and in individual residential neighborhoods. Here, social contacts were developed between neighbors Men used the *hammam* as a place for informal business discussions. The *hammam* also had a ritualistic significance, when it was reserved for a bride, her relatives, and friends before the wedding for a day-long celebration. Women went to the *hammam* to be ritually cleansed after giving birth. The *hammam* was also simply a place for recreation and relaxation.

MOTHER OF THE MAMLUKS

Nafisa al-Bayda, whose surname means 'the white,' was once a beautiful slave who gained wealth and influence through marriage to powerful Mamluks. Over the years, she acquired the name of Umm al-Mamalik ('mother of the Mamluks'). She entertained Napoleon himself in her home, and after his departure she was treated well by the British, although not by the Turks. Nafisa al-Bayda's influence on culture and history was not unlike that of her contemporaries Catherine the Great, Marie Antoinette, and Jane Austen. Her power later declined, and she died in 1816. She was buried with her first husband, 'Ali Bey, in the southern cemetery.

to much older, now ruined public baths) is still inscribed over the gate entrance. When the area became well known as a center for sugar and sweets, it acquired the name of **sukkariya**, or sugar house.

Opposite the **wikala** is the **Mosque–Madrasa of Sultan al-Mu'ayyad (61)**, built in 1415. Al-Mu'ayyad Shaykh was bought as a twelve-year-old Circassian slave by Barquq and rose rapidly in the Mamluk ranks. But prior to his becoming sultan in 1412, he had been imprisoned on this site, in the notorious prison called al-Shamali, and endured much suffering, so he vowed to destroy the prison and build a center of religious learning. He died in 1421. During his reign, the Mamluk empire reached its highest point.

In the fifteenth century, this **madrasa** became a prominent academic institution, with the most eminent scholars of the day teaching here. The façade of the building, raised to accommodate a row of shops, has a massive portal and dome over the mausoleum. The bronze doors were originally in the Sultan Hasan mosque. The mausoleum inside to the left contains the body of the founder and his son. The bent corridor leads to the sanctuary of the large congregational mosque. By the end of the nineteenth century, however, the mosque had fallen into disrepair and the courtyard was simply turned into a garden. On the eastern wall, the **qibla** is decorated in colored marble and geometric stucco patterns.

Bab Zuwayla (62), built in 1092, is the third of the Fatimid gates that remain standing (see also 2 and 4 above). This structure dominates the street, with the elegant twin towers of the al-Mu'ayyad mosque soaring over the gate. Both minarets are signed by Mu'allim (architect–builder) Muhammad ibn al-Qazzaz. On the south side of the gate, two rounded towers jut out, connected by a covered passageway over the large arched opening. To the west, the wall becomes part of the al-Mu'ayyad mosque, and to the east are the Fatimid ruins, concealed by dilapidated buildings. The minarets, which can be entered from the mosque, offer spectacular views of both inside and outside the walls.

The gate was named after the Fatimid soldiers from the Berber tribe of Zawila, who were billeted here at the time of its construction by Gawhar in 969, when only the elite were admitted in al-Qahira. In Mamluk times, the platform above the gate was the place from which sultans watched the elaborate **mahmal**, or caravan marking the start of the pilgrimage to Mecca. In

Bab Zuwayla from the entrance to the
Mosque-Madrasa of Sultan al-Mu'ayyad with
the dilapidated façade of the Wikala of
Nafisa al-Bayda to the left, once known as
sukkariya or "the house of sugar".

DUST, DEBRIS, AND GARBAGE

Cairo generates six thousand tons of waste a day. By comparison, London, with only half the population, produces 6,600 tons. Cairo's garbage collectors, a group of people called the *zabbalin*, remove waste only from the wealthiest districts, where there is a higher recycling value. The capital's cleaning authority also collects about a third of the city's garbage. The remaining thousand tons is left uncollected. Since much of historic Cairo's waste material has already been recycled, there is little incentive to pick up waste. Consequently, garbage and debris are widespread on the streets, on vacant plots, and on and around monuments.

the Ottoman period, the gate was also known as Bab al-Mitwalli because the *wali*, or commander of the security force, lived near here. It was also a place for public executions, and the heads of criminals were placed on stakes along the wall. It was here that the last Mamluk sultan, Tumanbay, was brutally hanged by Salim the Grim. In the nineteenth century, the gate was associated with Mitwalli al-Qutb, a resident saint who was known to perform miracles.

Outside the gate is the congested thoroughfare of Ahmad Mahir Street, creating a chaotic junction with al-Darb al-Ahmar to the east. Immediately opposite the gate, the cluster of impressive monuments continues. During the seventeenth century, this area was developed by the powerful Radwan Bey and was called the Qasabat Radwan, commonly known as the **Khiyamiya, or the Street of the Tent Makers (63)**, which is actually a continuation of al-Mu'izz Street. This area has been famous for its products since the eleventh century, when it provided the Fatimid armies with saddles and tents.

The small two-story building to the right on the other side of Ahmad Maher Street is the **Zawiya–Sabil of Farag ibn Barquq (64)**. This small Sufi establishment with panels of colored stone on the façade was intended for a *shaykh* to receive members of his brotherhood. It was built by Yusuf al-Ustadar in 1408. Originally, this building was much closer to Bab Zuwayla than at present, but was moved back to its present location in 1922 to widen the street and accommodate traffic.

On the east side, placed at an angle to the street, is the **Mosque of Salih Tala'i' (65)**, the last of the Fatimid mosques built in Cairo, constructed in 1160. When Salih Tala'i' built his mosque, the street level was some three meters lower than at present, as can be seen by the row of shops down behind the iron railings. A total of thirty-one shops were located on the front and sides of the mosque (but none on the *qibla* wall) as part of the endowment for the rent to pay for the upkeep. This was the first mosque to have shops provided in this manner. Because the mosque was above the shops it seemed as though it was hovering above the street; it had been conceived as a 'hanging' or 'suspended' building, a practice that was followed in successive centuries.

The porch entrance above the shops is a unique feature in Cairo, with a portico of five arches on classical pillars. Inside, a central courtyard is surrounded by colonnades on all four sides. The sanctuary has three rows of

Bab Zuwayla from outside the gate. Here is a chaotic atmosphere of buying and selling, of people shuffling to and fro along congested streets and alleyways.

THE *MAHMAL*

When Shagarat al-Durr (see page 64) made the pilgrimage to Mecca in royal state, she traveled in a richly decorated caravan. When she was unable to make the pilgrimage again, she sent the *mahmal*, or ornamental caravan, empty, but imbued with an aura of royal power. When al-Zahir Baybars became sultan in 1260, he maintained the custom of the empty *mahmal* at the head of the official caravan and it became an annual event. It contained copies of the Quran and was used to take a new *kiswa*, or cloth covers that were woven by Egyptian women every year for the Ka'ba in Mecca. This custom ceased in 1926.

columns (probably taken from pre-Islamic Christian churches), linked together by decorative tie beams. Above the decorated timber **minbar** is an opening for a **malqaf**.

The mosque was intended as the burial place for the head of al-Husayn, but the Fatimid caliph insisted that it should be buried in the palace (see also 41 above). Much restored and adopted through the centuries, the original mosque, except for the **qibla iwan**, was demolished in the early part of the twentieth century and rebuilt according to the original Fatimid plan.

Beyond these last two monuments is the splendid Street of the Tent Makers, the last remaining example of a traditional covered market in historic Cairo. Built in 1650 by Radwan Bey, the **amir al-hajj**. As he was responsible for the annual pilgrimage to Mecca, the **amir al-hajj** occupied one of the most prestigious offices in Mamluk and Ottoman times. Radwan Bey developed the district by providing various religious, secular, and commercial buildings and used the wealth of the Khiyamiya to fund not only part of the pilgrimage, but also the upkeep of educational and religious buildings.

This impressive market street is covered with a timber roof pierced by windows that allow shafts of light to penetrate down to the ground. Manufacturers of the tent fabrics still occupy the street, offering brightly colored patterns to cover walls and ceilings of the marquees used for weddings, funerals, and many community functions. Here craftsmen sit cross-legged on raised platforms in small stalls and make and sell the applique work, available in more subdued colors for tourists.

Beyond the shop fronts, however, this once magnificent structure now has little substance. Since 1992, even the covered street itself has been propped up by scaffolding. The living accommodation above the shops is now abandoned on the west side, although a few families still occupy the east side. To the southwest is Radwan Bey's palace, also largely derelict.

From the minarets of Bab Zuwayla is a fine
view of the open area leading to the Khiyamiya,
or Street of the Tent Makers, a continuation of
al-Mu'izz Street.

AMIR AL-HAJJ

Radwan Bey was *amir al-hajj* for twenty-five years, from 1631 to 1656. His duties were to organize the purchase of the supplies to accompany the caravan, to ensure proper distribution of food, and to provide protection to the pilgrims on their sacred journey to Mecca. The provision of grain and funds was also made to the Holy Cities of Mecca and Medina. Although the Ottoman Imperial Treasury made contributions, Radwan Bey donated large sums of money from his private revenues, including those from the Khiyamiya, to finance the trip. The ceremony of departure for the pilgrimage started outside Bab Zuwayla, near the Street of the Tent Makers.

A few paces to the south of the covered street, on the east side, are two buildings of interest. The first is the **Mosque of Mahmud al-Kurdi (66)**, built in 1395. It includes a madrasa and mausoleum. The stone dome is decorated with a zigzag pattern. A little further south, the second building, constructed in 1392, is the **Madrasa of Inal al-Yusufi (67)**, which also includes a mausoleum and a sabil–kuttab. The façades of the two buildings are similar, although the dome and minaret are transposed.

Walk back toward Bab Zuwayla. The vista down the covered street is distinctive, with the medieval gate at the center and the corbelled upper floors framing the view. Turn east into al-Darb al-Ahmar to continue to the final part of the route. During Fatimid times, the area outside Bab Zuwayla was inhabited by Greek troops. They were perceived as having red faces, from which al-Darb al-Ahmar ('the red district') is believed to derive its name.

Al-Darb al-Ahmar, the area between the city of al-Qahira and the Citadel, was once the site of Fatimid and Ayyubid cemeteries. When the Mamluks reinforced the Citadel as the seat of political, administrative, and military power, al-Darb al-Ahmar became a fashionable place to live. Many of the existing monuments date from the fourteenth century, when the Mamluks built their estates here to house their dependents, retainers, and even small private armies. They were soon followed by merchants, traders, and craftsmen who served their households. In the nineteenth century, Muhammad 'Ali's expansion of the Citadel created further opportunities for redevelopment in this area. Those who wished to be near the Citadel and the new ruler built many fine houses with projecting mashrabiya windows, many of which are now in a state of disrepair, or have disapeared completely.

Some two hundred meters along al-Darb al-Ahmar on a triangular site at the intersection with Abu Hurayra Street is the massive **Mosque of Qajmas al-Ishaqi (68)**. Built in 1480 by the head of Sultan Qaytbay's stables, it shows an ingenious way of utilizing this irregular site to the advantage of the mosque's symmetrical interior. It stands above the street level, which has risen considerably over the centuries, with shops on all sides. The room for ablutions and a sabil–kuttab are housed separately on a building across the street to the north that is linked to the mosque by a gallery with mashrabiya screens.

The soaring entrance, where another sabil is provided, is decorated with Quranic inscriptions and a marble panel of leaf forms in black, white, and red patterns. On the grille of the **sabil** is engraved the founder's blazon of three fields: a napkin on the upper, a cup between two horns in the middle, and another cup in the lower. The portal, with the tall minaret above, leads into a square central hall with a painted timber freeze. A lattice grille looks onto the domed mausoleum. The **qibla** wall is decorated with red and white marble, while the delicately carved **minbar** (pulpit) is inlaid with ivory. The high standards of workmanship in the decoration, carving, and gilt finishes make this one of the most remarkable mosques of Sultan Qaytbay's period.

A further hundred meters along al-Darb al-Ahmar is a fine nineteenth-century house with beautiful **mashrabiya** windows above; the ground floor is rather intrusively decorated with modern bathroom tiles. Customers at the café here are usually engrossed in intense games of backgammon. They are friendly and eager to talk about life in the Darb al-Ahmar district. You may like to stop here and have a short rest and a coffee or a soft drink.

The long winding street changes its name several times along this route, and this next part is called al-Tabbana Street. On the other side of the street is the **Ottoman Sabil–Kuttab of Muhammad Katkhuda Mustahfizan (69)**, built in 1677. This small building consists of essentially two façades making a shallow angle at the corner.

Adjoining the **sabil–kuttab** is the 1324 **Mosque of Ahmad al-Mihmandar (70)**, the oldest in the area. Ahmad was **mihmandar**, or head of protocol, and later became **amir al-hajj**. He died in 1332. The façade of this handsome building is divided by rows of calligraphic verses from the Quran and a foundation inscription. The tall dome is built of rendered brickwork. The minaret is Ottoman. In the northeast corner is the mausoleum with a fluted stone exterior.

Continue walking south, and further along the street on the right-hand side is one of the finest monuments of the fourteenth century, the **Mosque of Altinbugha al-Maridani (71)**, built in 1340. The amir Altibugha ('the golden bull') was the son-in-law of Sultan al-Nasir Muhammad. At the age of twenty-five, he was murdered in an attempt to gain al-Nasir's throne.

The plain façade of the mosque follows the curve of the street and is divided into a series of fenestrated panels with stalactite hoods. There is

THE *HAJJ*

It is the wish of every Muslim to undertake the *hajj*, or pilgrimage to Mecca. Each year, during the twelfth month of the Islamic calendar, between the eighth and thirteenth day, a vast migration of pilgrims of every race and color takes place, as they arrive together from all over the world in the same place at the same time. As a symbol of their devotion to God, pilgrims walk seven times around the black curtained Ka'ba, and many other sites associated with the Prophet and Isma'il are also visited. The *hajj* culminates in the Feast of Sacrifices, in commemoration of the sacrifice of Abraham.

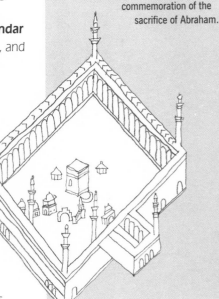

Al-Darb al-Ahmar is a long, winding street leading to the Citadel (although halfway along its name is changed to Bab al-Wazir). It became a fashionable place for the Mamluks to live.

also a Quranic inscription running along the top. The square first stage of the minaret has been drastically reduced, acting as a transition element between the building and the octagonal shaft above. The final stage of the minaret is capped by a small dome supported by slender columns. There are three clearly defined entrances to the mosque. The principal entrance is on the north façade, set in a vaulted recess, with a stalactite frieze. Inside, the mosque has an open courtyard surrounded by four porticoes. In the center of the courtyard is an octagonal timber fountain that was erected in Ottoman times. The beautifully carved and inlaid **qibla** arcade is separated from the rest of the mosque by an attractive **mashrabiya** screen. In front of the

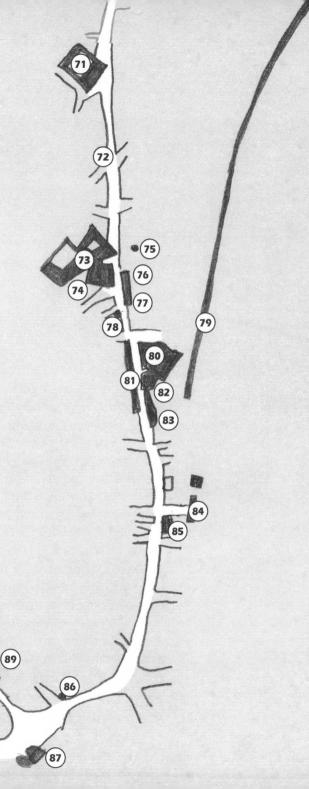

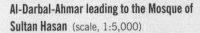

Al-Darbal-Ahmar leading to the Mosque of

Sultan Hasan (scale, 1:5,000)

71 Mosque of Altinbugha al-Maridani
72 *Zawiyat* 'Arif Pasha
73 House of Ahmad Katkhuda al-Razzaz
74 *Madrasat* Umm al-Sultan Sha'ban
75 Ayyubid minaret
76 *Sabil* and House of Ibrahim Agha
    Mustahfizan
77 Tomb of Ibrahim Khalifa Gindiyan
78 *Sabil* and Tomb of 'Umar Agha
79 Walls of Salah al-Din
80 Mosque of Ibrahim Agha Mustahfizan
81 *Rab'* of Tabbana
82 Mosque-Mausoleum of Amir Khayrbak
83 Palace of Alin Aq
84 Gate of Tarabay al-Sharifi
85 Mosque of Aytmish al-Bagasi
86 Mausoleum of Qansuh Abu Sa'id
87 Bab al-'Azab
88 Mosque of Mahmud Pasha
89 Mosque of Amir Akhur
90 Rifa'i Mosque
91 Mosque of Sultan Hasan
92 Open Air Café

MASHRABIYA

Timber was rare in Egypt and expensive. Consequently, it was used with care on buildings to richly decorate doors, ceilings, and windows and balconies, on which *mashrabiyas* were placed. *Mashrabiya* means 'drinking place,' and the term was used because porous earthenware jugs were placed near the latticed windows so that the incoming air would be cooled by the evaporation. From Mamluk times through to the nineteenth century, *mashrabiyas* were used as screens, partitions, and windows, providing gentle light, cool air, and privacy. *Mashrabiyas* have an aura of mystery because they were often used to isolate women from men, allowing the former to see, but not be seen.

qibla a small dome is supported by red granite columns of pharaonic origin. The building design was undertaken by Mu'allim ibn al-Suyufi, Sultan al-Nasir Muhammad's own architect.

Further south on the same side of the street is the unpretentious **Zawiyat 'Arif Pasha (72)**, built in 1866, on the corner with al-Tabbana Street and Suq al-Silah. This part of the main thoroughfare leading to the Citadel is named Bab al-Wazir.

Further along the same side of the street is the **House of Ahmad Katkhuda al-Razzaz (73)**, originally built in the fifteenth century by Sultan Qaytbay. A doorway dates Sultan Qaytbay's building to 1494. With its two courtyards, this rambling palace stretches from Bab al-Wazir Street to al-Tabbana Street. This palace was converted and expanded by Ahmad Katkhuda al-Razzaz in 1778. The huge palace, now sadly dilapidated within, contains several grand reception rooms, including a harem chamber. The entire palace developed through a process of addition and adaptation, culminating in Ottoman times in a transformed building with highly decorated rooms. On the Bab al-Wazir Street side, however, the building has a splendid façade of second-story windows.

Adjacent to Bayt al-Razzaz is the **Madrasat Umm al-Sultan Sha'ban (74)**, built in 1368. The sultan built it for his mother, Khwand Baraka ('Lady Blessing'), on making her pilgrimage to Mecca and Medina. It was built to teach only two rites, the Shafi'i and the Hanafi. The main features of the fortress-like façade is the grand entrance and the forty-five-degree turn of the building at the rear.

Opposite the *madrasa*, behind the street façade, a tall **Ayyubid Minaret (75)** dating from 1260 can be seen, although the mosque has now disappeared. Further along the street on the same side are a number of small monuments from the Ottoman period. Adjacent to the Ayyubid minaret is the **Sabil and House of Ibrahim Agha Mustahfizan (76)**, built in 1639 and 1652, respectively. Ibrahim Agha was a protégé of Radwan Bey and did much to revitalize this area in the seventeenth century. At the next corner is the **Tomb of Ibrahim Khalifa Gindiyan (77)**, built in 1593, while across the street is the 1652 **Sabil and Tomb of 'Umar Agha (78)**.

Directly opposite 'Umar Agha's tomb a short lane, Darb Shaghlan, leads to a local youth center, from where the **Walls of Salah al-Din (79)** can be seen.

The simple façade of Zawiyat 'Arif Pasha on the corner with al-Tabbana Street and Suq al-Silah provides a convenient link between important groups of monuments along the thoroughfare.

The imposing façade of the House of Ahmad Katkhuda al-Razzaz, with its splendid second-story windows, adjoins the fortress-like Madrasat Umm al-Sultan Sha'ban.

The walls, located to the east of al-Darb al-Ahmar district, stretch for more than a kilometer and are preserved from al-Azhar Road to the rear of the former palace of Alin Aq on Bab al-Wazir (see 81 below). Salah al-Din planned to unify al-Qahira, the Citadel, and al-Fustat with fortification walls, but he died before his plan was implemented. After the expansion of the population outside the city, the importance of the walls and gates as defenses diminished rapidly, yet to this day, the limits of the city to the east are defined by Salah al-Din's walls. Today, much of this wall is sadly neglected and parts of it are covered by refuse and debris.

Return to Bab al-Wazir Street and turn south, where another cluster of monuments is to be seen. In front is the **Mosque of Ibrahim Agha Mustahfizan (80)**. This mosque was founded in 1346 by Amir Shams al-Din Aqsunqur ('sun of religion, white falcon'), who was Sultan al-Nasir Muhammad's son-in-law. The mosque was restored in 1692 by the Ottoman officer Agha Mustahfizan, who had the interior walls covered in blue floral-patterned tiles imported from Istanbul and Damascus. Since that time, it has been known as the Blue Mosque.

The building is laid out around an open courtyard surrounded by four **iwan**s. A small dome sits over the **mihrab**. The fountain in the middle of the courtyard was added in 1412. The mosque contains

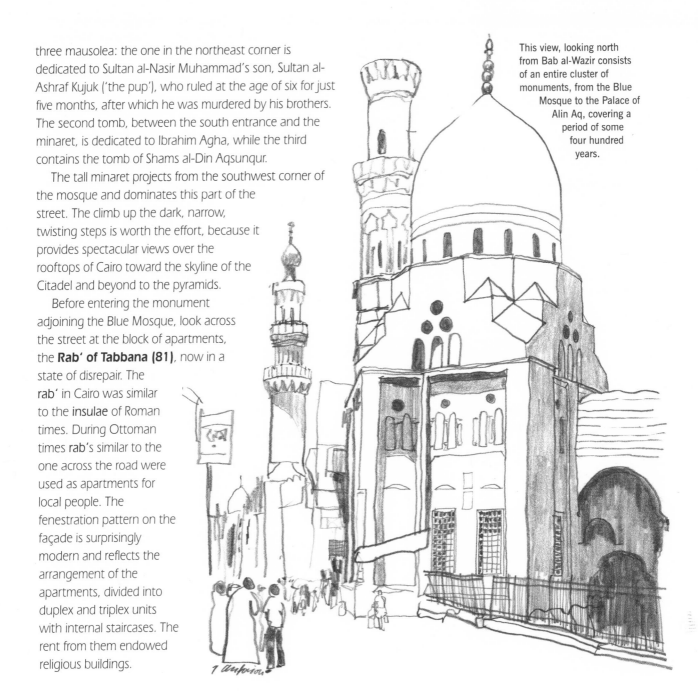

three mausolea: the one in the northeast corner is dedicated to Sultan al-Nasir Muhammad's son, Sultan al-Ashraf Kujuk ('the pup'), who ruled at the age of six for just five months, after which he was murdered by his brothers. The second tomb, between the south entrance and the minaret, is dedicated to Ibrahim Agha, while the third contains the tomb of Shams al-Din Aqsunqur.

The tall minaret projects from the southwest corner of the mosque and dominates this part of the street. The climb up the dark, narrow, twisting steps is worth the effort, because it provides spectacular views over the rooftops of Cairo toward the skyline of the Citadel and beyond to the pyramids.

Before entering the monument adjoining the Blue Mosque, look across the street at the block of apartments, the **Rab' of Tabbana (81)**, now in a state of disrepair. The rab' in Cairo was similar to the **insulae** of Roman times. During Ottoman times rab's similar to the one across the road were used as apartments for local people. The fenestration pattern on the façade is surprisingly modern and reflects the arrangement of the apartments, divided into duplex and triplex units with internal staircases. The rent from them endowed religious buildings.

This view, looking north from Bab al-Wazir consists of an entire cluster of monuments, from the Blue Mosque to the Palace of Alin Aq, covering a period of some four hundred years.

OTTOMAN TILES

Iznik, in northwest Anatolia (Turkey), became a center for ceramics patronized by the Ottoman court at the end of the fifteenth century. Patterns (most commonly floral ones, including roses, carnations, and tulips) were drawn on paper and sent by court artisans to be transformed into ceramic tiles in Iznik. The quality was very high, even when mass produced. By the mid-sixteenth century, the Iznik craftsmen were using a palette of blue, turquoise, sage green, and purple. Surprisingly, Ottoman tiles were not widely used in Cairo. In the Blue Mosque, however, Iznik tiles lavishly decorate one of the tomb chambers and the *qibla* wall.

There are numerous nineteenth- and early twentieth-century houses along Bab al-Wazir. Look out for this charming Art Nouveau window, with its elaborate shutters.

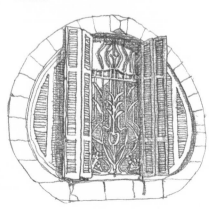

The monument next to the Blue Mosque is the **Mosque–Mausoleum of Amir Khayrbak (82)**. He betrayed his master Sultan al-Ghuri and defected to the Ottomans at the decisive battle near Aleppo in 1516, opening the door to the conquest of Egypt. As a result, he was made the first viceroy of the Ottomans in Egypt. From then on, he dressed in the Ottoman style and insisted on speaking in the Ottoman dialect.

The tomb was built in 1502, while the mosque and *sabil* attached to the mausoleum date from 1520, making the transition between the Mamluk and the Ottoman periods. The street façade is a rectangle, as compared to the irregular east side, and is clearly divided into three parts. On the northwest corner is the *sabil*, followed by the looming entrance to the mosque, then the tomb to the southwest, placed at an angle. The dome, topped with floral patterns, has simple triangular shoulders. The top section of the minaret is missing.

A few paces further south is the former **Palace of Alin Aq (83)**, originally built in 1293, which Khayrbak heavily restored as his residence. It is directly linked to the religious complex by stairs. The palace is now a ruin, however, and the only part that remains intact is the large round-arched entrance.

Continue walking south along Bab al-Wazir Street. In this part of the walk leading to the Citadel are numerous nineteenth- and early twentieth-century houses, which, although now dilapidated and neglected, retain an aura of grandeur and elegance, often with fine **mashrabiya** windows almost intact. There is also a strong community atmosphere here, not unlike a village, with one or two enticing bakeries and numerous cafés spilling out from the sidewalk onto the street.

The next turn on the left is Bab al-Turba Street (Gate of the Tomb), leading to the **Mausoleum, Sabil–Kuttab, and Gate of Tarabay al-Sharifi (84)**, built in 1503. Amir Tarabay was commander of the army of Mamluks in Egypt under Sultan al-Ghuri. The **sabil–kuttab** to the right of the gate once led to a **madrasa**, now demolished. The façade of the mausoleum, a large domed cube typical of the late Mamluk period, is composed of vertical panels crowned with stalactites. Large scrolls cover the corners of the transition zone to the dome, creating space for the triple windows on the façade. The tomb is all that remains of a much larger complex, now in a state of dilapidation and set in smoldering rubbish heaps. It was actually restored in 1905.

Return to Bab al-Wazir Street. At the corner with Bab al-Turba Street is the **Mosque of Aytmish al-Bagasi (85)**, built in 1383. This modest and compact complex was built by Sayf al-Din Aytmish al-Bagasi, a member of Sultan Farag ibn Barquq's entourage, who became regent for a short period in 1399. The sabil–kuttab, the first floor of which barely remains, is on the northwest corner, and a drinking trough is behind the mosque. The mausoleum is extended by a small dome boldly decorated with raised stone ribs.

Walk along the steeply rising Bab al-Wazir until you reach the walls of the massive Citadel at the junction with Bab al-Gadid Street. This road continues eastward up the incline, eventually leading to one of the main entrances to the Citadel. Follow the road southwest until you come to a small shrine by a simple café. This is the **Mausoleum of Qansuh Abu Sa'id (86)**, built in 1499.

Bab al-Turba Street leads to the Gate of Tarabay al-Sharifi. Beyond the gateway is the domed cube of the mausoleum.

When Qansuh eventually became sultan, he built a tomb much more impressive than this modest shrine in the eastern cemetery.

Continue west to one of the main entrances to the Citadel, **Bab al-'Azab (87)**, now locked. Built in 1754, the entrance is flanked by two massive half-round towers based on the design of Bab al-Futuh (see also 4 above). This part of the Citadel is actually from Muhammad 'Ali's period, and the surrounding walls were built in the nineteenth century. This particular gate, however, was added to the Citadel by Radwan Katkhuda as the entrance to the southern enclosure. It was used by the infantry corps that occupied the lower levels of the Citadel.

It was here, at the narrow passage inside the gate, that Muhammad 'Ali massacred the Mamluks, who had shown little regard for him. Muhammad 'Ali invited the most prominent Mamluks to a great banquet to honor his son at the Citadel. As they were leaving through the narrow passage leading to Bab al-Azab, the guards shot and killed all of them but one. Legend has it that Hasan Bey leapt with his horse over the ramparts, and escaped to Nubia.

The vast empty space in front of Bab al-'Azab, where many routes converge, has been converted into a traffic roundabout. When the Citadel was built, however, this area and Maydan Muhammad 'Ali to the southwest became the arena for polo games and horse races, military tournaments, religious processions, and elaborate ceremonies honoring the Mamluks.

Almost facing Bab al-'Azab is the free-standing **Mosque of Mahmud Pasha (88)**, built in 1568. Mahmud Pasha was Governor of Cairo for only two years, starting in 1565. He insisted on taking his executioner wherever he went with him. He often carried out death sentences on the spot on those who displeased him. He was finally assassinated by a sniper's bullet because of his cruel methods. The projecting tomb chamber

OTTOMAN TOMBS

Mosques developed in three distinct phases: those with a courtyard surrounded by arches on four sides; a specifically Egyptian type, with *iwan*s and a deeper portico on the side facing Mecca; and the Ottoman style, with a domed sanctuary and open porticoed courtyard. Monumental buildings within the city walls developed during the Fatimid period, then the Mamluks built massive tomb complexes within the city and at the cemeteries. After the Ottoman conquest of Egypt, the development of the cemeteries diminished. The Ottomans were buried in the courtyards of existing mausolea, as in the mosque of Aqsunqur, where Ibrahim Agha Mustahfizan's tomb adjoins the mosque.

imitates the Sultan Hasan Mosque, rather than the great mosques of Istanbul. The obvious Ottoman feature is the tall, pencil-thin minaret on the south corner.

To the east of the Mahmud Pasha mosque is the **Mosque of Amir Akhur (89)**, built in 1503. It was founded by Qanibay al-Sayfi, also known as al-Rammah ('the lancer'), and Amir Akhur Kabir, or Grand Master of the Horse, during the reign of Sultan al-Ghuri. Significantly, the horse market and stables were originally located nearby, below the Citadel.

The small Mausoleum of Qansuh Abu Sa'id, along the steep side street following the walls of the Citadel, is surrounded by irregular workshops and makeshft cafés, all part of the busy life of the community.

The change in the terrain necessitated the splitting up of the building and placing the **sabil–kuttab** at the lower level of the complex. The mosque was reached by a long flight of steps. The minaret, with double finials, is typical of the late Mamluk period. The stone dome with its triangular corner supports is carved with arabesque patterns.

Looking northwest is a canyon-like pedestrian street created by the juxtaposition of two massive buildings. The monumental structure on the right is the relatively new **Rifa'i Mosque (90)**, founded in 1819, but not completed until 1912. Its site was a former **zawiya**, which was acquired and demolished by Princess Khushyar, the daughter of the Khedive Isma'il.

The mosque was built with tombs for Shaykh 'Ali al-Rifa'i, a saint buried on the site before the mosque was built, and Shaykh 'Abd Allah al-Ansari, a companion of the Prophet. It also contains the mausolea for Princess Khushyar and her descendants. King Fu'ad, who ruled between 1917 and 1936, and his mother are also buried here, along with Farouk, the last king of Egypt, and the last shah of Iran, Muhammad Pahlavi.

This panoramic view encompasses a whole range of monuments, from the majestic Sultan Hasan Mosque on the left, through the Rifa'i Mosque, the Mosque of Amir Akhur, and the Mosque of Mahmud Pasha to Bab al-'Azab, one of the entrances to the Citadel.

The building was designed by Husayn Pasha Fahmi, while the overwhelming, high quality decorations compiled from Mamluk sources were carried out by Max Herz, chief architect to the famous Comité de Conservation de Monuments de l'Art Arabe, which was founded in 1881 to preserve Islamic monuments.

Walk across to the west side of the pedestrian street, and you step back six hundred years in history. The **Mosque of Sultan Hasan (91)**, the finest Muslim monument existing in Egypt, was built between 1356 and 1363, a time when Europe was poised for a new era in art and architecture. The construction of Florence Cathedral, marking the beginning of the Renaissance, was being carried between 1296 and 1462, with the dome by Fillipo Brunelleschi built between 1420 and 1436.

The Sultan Hasan mosque is at least twice as large as the average mosque in Cairo and one of the largest in the world. It was so monumental in scale that sometimes it acted as a fortress during Mamluk conflicts in their pursuit of power. In 1391, its roof was used to hurl projectiles at rivals in the Citadel. Some hundred years later, the mosque was bombarded when it served as a refuge for Tumanbay, the last Mamluk sultan (see also 61 above).

The impressive *dikka*, or platform, in the Mosque of Sultan Hasan, is used by chanters of the Quran to project their voices onto the congregation in the courtyard.

LE COMITÉ

In 1880, the Egyptian Government began to assemble the loose pieces of Cairo's monuments in a corner of the al-Hakim mosque, to save them from the hands of mainly European antiquarians. In 1882, a number of foreign enthusiasts formed the Committee of the Preservation of Arab Monuments and was recognized as an official body. Known in Cairo as the Comité, its duties were to make an inventory of the monuments and preserve and maintain them accurately. In 1903, the material gathered in al-Hakim mosque was placed in the newly built museum, now called the Museum of Islamic Art. The Comité was abolished in 1952.

The irregular outline of this vast building probably follows the sites of earlier structures (see plan on p 6). Sultan Hasan was able to build this imposing monument from the estates of those who died of the Black Death when it struck Egypt in 1348. These estates provided large funds to the treasury, which then became available for royal endowments.

The plan falls into three distinct parts (see also plan on page 6). First, on the north side (where the ticket office is located), is the area used for commercial purposes. Now obscured, this area was used to obtain rents to ensure the upkeep of the building. Second is the transitional area, offset by thirty degrees from the main courtyard. The third part is the mosque itself.

The mosque is a cruciform plan, the first in Cairo, with a central courtyard and four **iwan**s. At each of the corners of the courtyard is a four- to five-story **madrasa**, corresponding to one of the four Sunni Orthodox rites, and each with an **iwan** for teaching. The **qibla iwan** is decorated with stucco friezes inscribed with a long Kufic script in a lacework of plaster. This **iwan** also contains a marble **minbar**, one of the finest in Cairo, and an impressive **dikka**. Long chains held enameled glass lamps. Some of the original ones are preserved in the Museum of Islamic Art, while others are to be found in the Victoria and Albert Museum in London.

Behind the **qibla iwan**, entered through a set of doors (the one on the right is original), is the square mausoleum. It is built on a grand scale, and is the largest in Cairo. Completed two years after Sultan Hasan's death, it was never occupied by him, since he was murdered, and his body mysteriously disappeared. Two of his sons are buried here, however. The location of this lofty and somber mausoleum was chosen for maximum visibility from the urban surroundings and is designed to stand out from the rest of the building. Internally, it is situated behind the **qibla**, granting it some religious significance. Its imposing location would have been further extended by two minarets at the south corners of the mosque, although only one survives. The dome was rebuilt in Ottoman times, after its collapse in 1660 as a result of an earthquake.

The massive effect is created by the soaring stone façades and its overhanging cornice running along the top of the walls. Vertical bays are also used for openings, making the walls look even taller. The huge portal with its stalactite arch adds considerably to the building's greatness. A further two minarets were intended on either side of the portal to further emphasize the entrance. In 1360, one of the minarets collapsed, killing three hundred people. Consequently, the construction of the other tower was abandoned.

The monumental simplicity of this building is overwhelming. The transition from the entrance to the courtyard through the narrow passage is one from subdued darkness to bright sunlight. The peaceful interior is an expression of grandeur, and you should spend a little time in this majestic building to absorb its aura of greatness.

When you finally emerge into the street again, between the tall buildings, you may wish to have a soft drink at the **Open Air Café (92)**. This is located in the garden at the rear next to the ticket office. You can relax and contemplate at your leisure the long route of this walk in one of the most remarkable historic cities. Take your time, for the waiters are unlikely to be in a hurry to serve you.

SULTAN HASAN

Al-Nasir al-Hasan was the son of the great builder Sultan al-Nasir Muhammad. Hasan first became sultan of Egypt in 1347, at the age of thirteen. He was deposed four years later in favor of one of his younger brothers. After three years of seclusion, he was restored as sultan until his assassination in 1362, at the age of twenty-eight. Throughout his reign he remained a puppet in the hands of powerful amirs, although he built this majestic monument, colossal in scale and bold in conception.

GLOSSARY

Amir A military commander

Arabesque Ornament based on vegetal forms in continuous interlacing patterns

Bab Gate or door

Bayt House

Caliph The 'Successor,' the religious and political leader of the Muslim community

Corbel A projecting bracket to support another structure

Darb A thoroughfare or path

Dikka A raised platform in a mosque used for Quranic recitals, chants and calls to prayer

Hadith The collected words of the Prophet Muhammad, a traditional source of Islamic law

Hara Neighborhood, particularly a small, closed one inhabited by members of the same tribe or trade

Hajj The pilgrimage to Mecca

Hammam A bath, public or private

Haramlik 'The forbidden area,' or women's quarters

Hawd Public trough for watering animals

Hawsh or Hosh A courtyard

Iwans The vaulted spaces around the courtyard of a mosque or a madrasa

Ka'ba The large cubic construction associated with the sanctuary in Mecca

Khan A hostel associated with merchants

Khanqah A hostel for Sufis

Kufic The earliest style of Arabic script

Kuttab A Quranic school for young boys

Madrasa A theological school where the four primary schools of Islamic law were taught

Malqaf A north-facing wind catcher to cool the interior of a building

Maq'ad An open, arch-fronted sitting area, usually on the first floor overlooking a courtyard

Maristan A hospital

Mashrabiya A decorative timber lattice screen

Maydan An open space, a garden or square, originally a polo ground

Merlon A parapet with alternating raised parts and indentations

Mihrab The niche that indicates the direction of Mecca for prayer

Minaret A tower from which the call to prayer was given

Minbar A pulpit

Mulid A religious festival

Muqarnas An ornamental arrangement of multi-tiered niches on domes, squinches or portals; also called 'stalactites'

Pendentive A triangular area formed by cutting away corners so that a square building can accommodate a dome

Qa'a A large reception room

Qadi A Muslim judge

Qasaba The city's commercial street

Qasr A castle or palace

Qibla The direction Muslims face to pray, or the wall in a mosque facing that direction

Quran The scriptures of Islam

Rab' An apartment building

Sabil A public drinking fountain

Sahn The central courtyard of a mosque

Salamlik The 'greeting area,' or the men's room

Shi'i Referring to the smaller branch of Islam that believes in the righteousness of 'Ali, the Prophet's son-in-law

Sufi A Muslim ascetic

Sultan An independent ruler of territories

Sunni Referring to Orthodox Islam, as opposed to Shi'i Islam

Suq A traditional market

Takiya The Ottoman equivalent of a Sufi hostel

Waqf Land or property perpetually endowed to a pious institution, the income from which is used to pay for the building's upkeep

Wazir A principal minister of administration

Wikala A warehouse for the storage of goods, with upper floors for rent

Zawiya A residence for a particular Sufi order

The *Sabil-Kuttab* of Nafisa al-Bayda (see also page 85).

INDEX

Figures in bold type refer to illustrations